Literary Intellectuals

Studies on Themes and Motifs in Literature

Horst S. Daemmrich
General Editor

Vol. 117

PETER LANG
New York • Washington, D.C./Baltimore • Bern
Frankfurt • Berlin • Brussels • Vienna • Oxford

Abdulla Al-Dabbagh

Literary Intellectuals

East and West

PETER LANG
New York • Washington, D.C./Baltimore • Bern
Frankfurt • Berlin • Brussels • Vienna • Oxford

Library of Congress Cataloging-in-Publication Data

Al-Dabbagh, Abdulla.
Literary intellectuals: East and West / Abdulla Al-Dabbagh.
p. cm. — (Studies on themes and motifs in literature; v. 117)
Includes bibliographical references.
1. Criticism. 2. Intellectuals. 3. Intellectual life. 4. Literature
and society. 5. Modernism (Literature). I. Title.
PN81.A39   801'.95—dc23   2012029479
ISBN 978-1-4331-2142-5 (hardcover)
ISBN 978-1-4539-0960-7 (e-book)
ISSN 1056-3970

Bibliographic information published by **Die Deutsche Nationalbibliothek**.
Die Deutsche Nationalbibliothek lists this publication in the "Deutsche
Nationalbibliografie"; detailed bibliographic data is available
on the Internet at http://dnb.d-nb.de/.

The paper in this book meets the guidelines for permanence and durability
of the Committee on Production Guidelines for Book Longevity
of the Council of Library Resources.

© 2013 Peter Lang Publishing, Inc., New York
29 Broadway, 18th floor, New York, NY 10006
www.peterlang.com

Printed in Germany

CONTENTS

PREFACE AND ACKNOWLEDGMENTS

The first seven of the essays collected in this book deal with Western intellec-tuals; in fact, with a largely British tradition of cultural criticism. The last three essays deal with Arab intellectuals and Arab literary and cultural concerns.

Written over the period of some thirty years, one of these essays was published in 1987 and four were published in the first decade of this century in academic journals. The rest, again written in different periods, have not been published before. Six of these papers were delivered at international conferences.

I would like to thank the editors of *Neohelicon* for the permission to reprint "The Literary and Cultural Criticism of Raymond Williams" (read at the Colloquium of the International Comparative Literature Association, "Literature and Values", held at the University of Sussex, UK, August 1985), the Editor-in-Chief of the *International Journal of Arabic/English Studies* for his permission to reprint "Poetics of Exile and Identity: The Case of Modern Iraqi Poetry" (read at the Sixth British Council Symposium on English Studies in Europe, held in Delphi, Greece, 7–13 September, 2003), "Power and the Radical Arab Intellectual" (read at the Eighth International Symposium on Comparative Literature, "Power and the Role of the Intellectual", held at the English Department, Cairo University, Egypt, 22–24 November, 2005), and

"Islamophobia and the Intellectuals" (read at the "Fear of the Other" Colloquium organized by the Sorbonne/Abu Dhabi University in Abu Dhabi and Al-Ain, United Arab Emirates, 17–19 March 2009)), and the editors of the *Journal of Mediterranean Studies* for their permission to reprint "Mediterraneanism in Modern Arab Cultural Thought" (read at the Sixth International Mediterranean Studies Association Conference, "The Mediterranean and Central Europe", held at the Central European University, Budapest, Hungary, 28–31 May, 2003). "Radical, Renegades, Pundits and Imposters" was delivered at the 2011 European Association for Commonwealth Literature and Language Studies conference, "Under Construction: Gateways and Walls", held at Bogazici University in Istanbul, Turkey, 26–30 April, 2011.

Once again, I dedicate this book to my wife and children, without whose support these essays would never be written.

I would also like to record my thanks, once again, to the College of Humanities and Social Sciences in the United Arab Emirates University for it generous support, and to Ms Jackie Pavlovic, production supervisor for Peter Lang for her efforts, toward the publication of these essays.

· 1 ·

THREE FIGURES: T.S. ELIOT, F.R. LEAVIS, GEORGE ORWELL

T.S. Eliot and Culture

One clear example of Eliot's cultural elitism is his views on education. Aside from his opposition to secular education in general and his open advocacy of a strictly religious education[1]—obviously a form of elitism—Eliot has also argued against the very principle of *democratic* education. Thus, in his *Notes towards the Definition of Culture*, he says:

> The prospect of a society ruled and directed only by those who have passed certain examinations or satisfied tests devised by psychologists is not reassuring . . . Furthermore, the ideal of a uniform system such that no one capable of receiving higher education could fail to get it, leads imperceptibly to the education of too many people, and consequently to the lowering of standards to whatever this swollen number of candidates is able to reach.[2]

In addition, Eliot passionately defended that epitome of elitist education, the public school system, as well as the aristocratic, and by that time rather anachronistic, character of Oxford and Cambridge universities.[3]

Another manifestation of Eliot's elitism is his antagonism to minority groups and minority cultures. In this, he is clearly a cultural segregationist in exactly the sense used to describe the policies of the southern states of the US or the apartheid system in South Africa.[4]

Similarly, there are rudiments of a wider historical "theory" in Eliot's writings, as exemplified by his views on such events as the French Revolution[5] or the American Civil War[6]. Very simply the Eliotic interpretation of history amounts to the rejection of all "egalitarian" moments in modern European history from the Reformation down to the modern rise of liberalism and "mass democracy". All this for Eliot is the history of decline and disaster. It is no doubt an excessively pessimistic example of the organic myth of an imagined aristocratic community tied together by the bonds of race, religion and soil that has had to suffer the onslaught of successive egalitarian and democratic movements. But for Eliot there clearly was no hope, except through such 'revitalizing' movements as the fascist *Action Francaise*[7] for which he often expressed his admiration.

Furthermore, Eliot was not only a religious bigot and a racist; he was also very much a sexist. In all his writings, there is the constant image of woman as a mere sexual object. Either that, or she is regarded as just a mechanism for breeding children.[8] In fact, this is the one point, i.e. Eliot's sexism, on which even the admirers of Eliot, such people as the critic F.R. Leavis, who generally sympathized with his views, tend to agree.

Eliot's understanding of the history of English literature betrays the same elitism and anti-democratic bias. There can, in fact, be no justification for his vehement rejection of such classic writers of English as Milton, Burns, Shelley, Dickens and Shaw except their social and political sympathies—republicanism, democracy, liberalism, and socialism—which Eliot so intensely hated. Such judgments, based upon sheer prejudice, are invariably expressed in cryptic, sophomoric language. They are, as a rule, unsubstantiated and not based on any rational argument. Moreover, they often conceal, particularly in the case of the poets, the antipathy towards the writers' beliefs by a dismissal on artistic grounds.

Perhaps the best word that sums up Eliot's cultural elitism is Tradition, which for him has very specific connotations. It is a term that bridges the realms of culture, literature and politics. What it means, essentially, is an ordered, hierarchic system of subordination whereby the individual is subsumed in a higher system based on degree and on gradation. A royalist in politics, a classicist in art and a catholic in religion is how Eliot once described himself. This is the crux of Eliot's cultural theorizing—the advocacy of an elitist, minority culture under the pretence of defending tradition, order, cultural gradation or what have you:

What is important is a structure of society in which there will be, from 'top' to 'bottom', a continuous gradation of cultural levels: it is important to remember that we should not consider the upper levels as possessing more culture than the lower, but as representing a *more* conscious culture and a greater specialization of culture.[9]

This is Eliot's initial argument. He develops it further by saying that the so-called upper and lower cultures inter-act and enrich each other. All this, however, is mere subterfuge and pretence at argument. Eliot's position is simply that the masses are incapable of the higher culture and should be given no encouragement in that direction.[10] In fact, it is this very diffusion of culture, this leveling and egalitarianism, this democratization of education, that Eliot finds to be the very basis for the destruction of culture:

If, for instance, he (the reader) finds it shocking that culture and equalitarianism should conflict, if it seems monstrous to him that anyone should have 'advantages of birth'—I do not ask him to change his faith, I merely ask him to stop paying lip-service to culture.[11]

Eliot's cultural elitism was strongly connected to his elitist political outlook. Here there can be no justification for splitting the cultural theorist from the political theorist or even from the poet and the literary critic. Elitism—the rejection of democracy and the insistence on the "advantages of birth"—permeated Eliot's concern in all *three* areas. In fact, Eliot's outlook together with his literary criticism and his poetry are so much of a piece that he should be regarded as the opposite of the grand nineteenth century literary figures—like Balzac or Tolstoy—whose literary products quite often *undercut* their political allegiances and philosophic positions. They were artists first and propagators of ideas second. Or, to put it in another way, their devotion to the truth of literary representation quite often refuted their cherished philosophic ideals which were at variance with the real course of events. Eliot, on the other hand, was a propagandist first and an artist second. He started out from certain basic philosophic and political assumptions and *utilized* his art to the service of "proving" them over and over again. Even in terms of output, his other writings outweigh his poetry and his plays. For this reason, Eliot is the very type of figure whose views cannot be separated from his creative work—in direct opposition to the strategy used by the school of so-called "New Criticism" who took the guidelines for their critical approach from Eliot's own work, and endeavored to apply them to modern literature. It is almost as if Eliot's early "revolutionary" poetry (*The Waste Land*) and criticism (*The Sacred Wood* essays) were written in order to make a "name" for himself which, as he himself

later admitted, was essential before he could have a ready platform to pontifi-
cate from on various social and political issues.

From poetry and criticism, Eliot moved more and more towards culture,
politics and religion. In the area of culture—which is the specific concern
of this essay—his elitism, as we have said, was closely linked to his general
political outlook. Take, for example, his insistence that culture and democracy
(equalitarianism, as he called it) could not be reconciled and that culture and
advantages of birth could not be separated, and compare it with the terms he
uses to outline his political position:

> We may assume, I think, that in a society so articulated the practice of politics and
> an active interest in public affairs would not be the business of everybody, or of every-
> body to the same degree, and that not everybody should concern himself, except at
> moments of crisis, with the conduct of the nation as a whole. In a healthily *regional*
> society, public affairs would be the business of everybody, or of the great majority, only
> within very small social units; and would be the business of a progressively smaller
> number of men in the larger units within which the smaller were comprehended. In a
> healthily *stratified* society, public affairs would be a responsibility not equally borne: a
> greater responsibility would be inherited by those who inherited special advantages,
> and in whom self-interest and interest for the sake of their families ('a stake in the
> country') should cohere with public spirit.[12]

The terms are almost identical. Just as the masses should not aspire to the
appreciation of "the more conscious part of culture", so must they not concern
themselves with public affairs above a certain trivial level. Just as they cannot succeed in the cultural endeavor, in fact, their efforts would only result in
"adulterating" and "cheapening" culture according to Eliot, so can they not
possibly play a role in public affairs or represent the nation because having
no "special advantages" of wealth and birth, they do not have a "stake in the
country" and, therefore, could not truly represent it. Eliot has no hesitation
in expressing his class solidarity with the aristocracy and with those who, by
his criteria, "have a stake in the country". That much is clear. He is, however,
distinguished from the common-run apologist of the ruling classes in that he
openly rejects the mechanics of bourgeois democracy[13] in favor of an elitist,
aristocratic and proto-fascist rule. The outlines of Eliot's vision of the "new
order" that would replace the decaying class society *as well as* check the tendency toward a socialist classless society, is clearly described below:

> Whilst it is generally supposed that class; in any sense which maintains associations
> with the past, will disappear, it is now the opinion of some of the most advanced
> minds that some qualitative differences between individuals must still be recognised,

and that superior individuals must be formed into suitable groups, endowed with appropriate powers, and perhaps with varied emoluments and honours. Those groups, formed of individuals who opt for powers of government and administration, will direct the public life of the nation; the individuals composing them will be spoken of as 'leaders'. There will be groups concerned with art, and groups concerned with philosophy, as well as groups consisting of men of action; and these groups are what we call *elites*.[14]

There is then not much of an argument on the topic of culture in Eliot's writings. Even in his *Notes towards the Definition of Culture*, a work devoted to this theme, where, as the title at first suggests, he assumes the role of the researcher, there is nothing beyond the re-affirmation of elitist rule and elitist culture supported now by a few pages from the sociology of Karl Manheim. Other than this, the work is built around a number of assertions, prejudices and false assumptions. They key idea for Eliot, which he presents almost as a great discovery, is that culture is "the way of life of a particular people living together in one place."[15]

This is asserted several times throughout the work, in the same grand manner.[16] It is, of course, no more than the preliminary concept of national life, and adds nothing to it. In the definition then—ostensibly the object of the exercise—there is a platitude; the real "originality" of Eliot lies in the corollary to the definition—that is the belief in high and low culture, in the culture of the masses and the culture of the elite which is really the crux of the matter and the primary prejudice for him.

Aside from this there is not much to say about Eliot's argument. The only way to talk about the rest of the work—and this is the method all writers on Eliot's so-called cultural theorizing have invariably followed—is to list a series of his assertions on the various topics, which all in the end, without even the resemblance of rational argument, are merely part and parcel of basic tendencies and prejudices. For example, to list them in order of appearance, there is his obviously false concept of the inseparability of culture and religion:

> The first important assertion is that no culture has appeared or developed except together with a religion: according to the point of view of the observer, the culture will appear to be the product of the religion, or the religion the product of the culture[17] . . .

> Yet there is an aspect in which we can see religion as the *whole way of life* of a people . . . And we have to face the strange idea that what is part of our culture is also a part of our *lived* religion.[18]

Then, there is his cultural pessimism and "doctrine" of decline;

> We can assert with some confidence that our own period is one of decline; that the standards of culture are lower than they were fifty years ago; and that the evidences of this decline are visible in every department of human activity.[19]

Cultural elitism;

> The writer himself is not without political conviction and prejudices . . . What I try to say is this: Here are what I believe to be essential conditions for the growth and for the survival of culture. If they conflict with any passionate faith of the reader—if, for instance, he finds it shocking that culture and equalitarianism should conflict, if it seems monstrous to him that anyone should have 'advantages of birth'—I do not ask him to change his faith, I merely ask him to stop paying lip-service to culture.[20]

Elite rule:

> It is now the opinion of some of the most advanced minds that some qualitative differences between individuals must still be recognised and that superior individuals must be formed into suitable groups, endowed with appropriate powers, and perhaps with varied emoluments and honours. Those groups, formed of individuals apt for powers of government and administration, will direct the public life of the nation; the individuals composing them will be spoken of as 'leaders'.[21]

This is the basic position, and notice how invariably it is introduced, as can be seen in the examples cited, by words like "assertion", "opinion", "prejudice", etc. In order to complete the picture, here are a few more of Eliot's "views" on a number of related topics. For example, democracy:

> A democracy in which everybody had an equal responsibility in everything would be oppressive for the conscientious and licentious for the rest.[22]

Colonialism is implicitly defended when it is put in terms of "higher" and "lower" cultures, and not in terms of economic exploitation and political oppression:

> The colonial problem is that of the relation between an indigenous native culture and a foreign culture, when a higher foreign culture has been imposed, often by force, upon a lower.[23]

> To point to the damage that has been done to native cultures in the process of imperial expansion is by no means an indictment of empire itself, as the advocates of imperial dissolution are only too apt to infer.[24]

And, finally, a series of really laughable statements, made of nothing but reactionary prejudices, on education, with which this section ends for the amusement of the reader:

> To be trained, taught or instructed above the level of one's abilities and strength may be disastrous; for education is a strain, and can impose greater burdens upon a mind than that the mind can bear. Too much education, like too little education, can produce unhappiness.[25]

> A high average of general education is perhaps less necessary for a civil society than is a respect for learning.[26]

> There is no doubt that in our headlong rush to educate everybody, we are lowering our standards.[27]

F.R. Leavis and *Scrutiny*

The literary and cultural criticism of F.R. Leavis cannot be separated from the magazine *Scrutiny*, which he edited for twenty years and which he described as the product of the teaching of English literature at Cambridge University.

Now if we remember that English literature was first introduced as an independent academic discipline during the First World War and from the purely chauvinistic and imperialist impulse of fighting "Teutonic thought", on the one hand, and "Bolshevism", on the other, then we can be put in the right perspective from which to estimate the role that *Scrutiny* came to play in the thirties and the forties.

From the first issue *Scrutiny* declared in its manifesto that it was going to be more than a purely literary journal and would concern itself directly with general social and cultural issues. Together with Leavis's early pamphlet, *Mass Civilization and Minority Culture*, this set the tone for the periodical's basic attitudes: attacks on what it regarded as mass culture, i.e. the popular press, advertisements, best sellers, and so on, together with all kinds of purely technological advance which it condemned under the label of industrialism. In their place, it advocated "high culture" which consisted mainly of the works of the reactionary modernist writers, particularly those of T. S. Eliot and D. H. Lawrence, plus a selective interpretation of the history of English literature to endorse the reactionary elitism and yearning for an "organic", hierarchical, pastoral community.

The absurdity of these positions is revealed even on the strictly cultural ground. For example, *Scrutiny* opposed the cinema as an art form with popular and commercial appeal, dismissing it contemptuously as 'the art-form of democracy'. It regarded those intellectuals who were interested in films as traitors to the cause, and it stated categorically that no film could ever achieve the artistic status of a novel or a poem. Almost all the contributors to the journal regarded the cinema as a culturally disruptive force, and their leader, Leavis, in his characteristically paranoiac way, described it, together with the radio and the motor car, as the evil products of industrialism.

The outline of British social and cultural history offered by *Scrutiny* is one of basic decline for which from the Elizabethan epoch onwards two major movements have been primarily responsible: The English Revolution and the Industrial Revolution. As a result, according to the Scrutineers, a homogeneous, "organic", agricultural community has been replaced by an atomized, mechanized, industrial waste land. The rest is familiar. The enemy is the machine, mass society, urbanism, and all the rest (films, radio, the press, etc). In literary terms, they endorsed Eliot's myth of a so-called "dissociation of sensibility", supposed to have occurred sometime in the 17th century, as the primary cause of the steady decline in literature. This was seized upon as a convenient "concept" for fighting radicalism and for propagating blatantly reactionary ideology among several generations of students of literature.

Moreover, *Scrutiny's* prejudices were not merely a question of innocent literary criticism. As has been pointed out, its ambitions were as much social and cultural as literary. And for this, it had a fully thought-out strategy which consisted of organizing an elite that was to become the guardian of high culture and of utilizing the instruments of the small periodical and of the Cambridge School of English for that purpose. For this, it postulated the absurd theory of English literature as the "center" of modern education and of literary criticism as the commanding height from which all humanistic studies should he directed. For two decades, the journal concentrated its energy and devoted most of its pages to literature to the exclusion of other areas as well as of nearly all other arts. And it narrowed that area even further by devoting its attention to English literature almost to the total exclusion of all other literatures. Yet, from this narrow, parochial, chauvinistic and reactionary standpoint, it claimed for itself the position of the center as well as the pinnacle of all human culture.

Thus *Scrutiny* took it upon itself to initiate a crusade against low standards, base values and cultural barbarism. All this was invariably dressed up in very solemn, moral terms, and in an offensive holier-than-thou fashion. In a totally arbitrary way, it set out to distinguish between the Good and the Bad both in old as well as new writing. Milton, Shelley and Dickens were the bad writers; Marvell, Keats and George Eliot, the good. The Bloomsbury Group—Virginia Woolf, Lytton Strachey, E.M. Forster—and the Oxford poets of the thirties—Auden, Spender, et al were condemned, while Eliot and Lawrence were praised to the skies. All this, however, was done in all seriousness and under the guise of carefully thought-out, morally "felt" arguments and "close attention" to the texts. When prejudices changed, however, e.g., when Eliot became not so good and Forster not so bad, or when a particular Lawrence novel changed from a masterpiece to trashy writing, or vice versa—no explanation was offered.

The separation of literature and literary criticism from other fields of study by postulating it as the centre of all the humanities also provided the pretext for refusing to explain the criteria on which *Scrutiny*'s literary judgments were based. Literature was declared to be above all the other disciplines, and therefore it was forbidden to use, for the purposes of literary criticism, terms driven from any other discipline. Sociology, politics, history, philosophy were out. The absurd cult of literature as nothing but literature was set up and the method of so-called close textual reading—or practical criticism—was "discovered." All this was no more than a new form of aestheticism and a new art-for-art's sake ideology disguised this time in fiery, moral terms and crusading, cultural saber-rattling.

Thus *Scrutiny* can be said to have accomplished its aims. Under the cloak of a radical and iconoclastic moralism, it managed to spread more reactionary poison and over a wider space and a longer period of time than any other literary and cultural organ in the first half of the century in Britain. This is no mean "achievement", which, incidentally, would have been *impossible* without the support of the ruling establishment to which *Scrutiny* often set itself up as an antagonist. The evidence can also be seen in the celebration it has received in recent years where *all* the issues of the journal have been re-published in twenty volumes, and a steady flood of books and articles about it and about its editor has been coming out ever since. One recent study, published revealingly by the New Left Review publishing house, describes the journal as "an ineffaceable image in the memory of national culture" and calls the whole epoch 'the moment of Scrutiny',[28] which it also chooses as the title of the study. The argument and, in fact, the very production of such a book from such a source, is an affirmation that Leavis is the link between the reactionary cultural elitism of Eliot and Lawrence and the pseudo-socialist cultural chauvinism of the New Left, particularly of Raymond Williams. The inheritance of the English

New Left—Raymond Williams, Perry Anderson and E.P. Thompson—of such a reactionary legacy and, in fact, their open identification, celebration and assimilation of it will be discussed in the following chapters.

Ironically, the pseudo-left's chief reason for celebrating its newly-found hero, Leavis—in the sense that only now with the tide turning right-wards has it dared to come out openly for him although it always shared basic assumptions from the start—which is the fact that he is a genuine, unadulterated English product, is misconceived. For, in fact, Leavis's thought, however hard he may have tried to conceal it, is *derived*. And it is derived from European, and largely German, origins. In particular his debts are to German vitalist philosophy, to Bergson, to Nietzsche, to Tonnies and, in fact, to the whole course of the reactionary trend in Germany philosophy in the last quarter of the 19th Century and the first decades of the 20th and most prominently to the work of Oswald Spengler. As for the claim to "Englishness" that it may make via Eliot and Lawrence, the very choice of those two refutes the argument. Their thinking and basic outlook is so obviously "non-English"—in the case of Lawrence it is German and Nietzschean and in that of Eliot it is Latin, particularly French, and strongly dominated by Charles Maurras. So it is the ultimate irony that the English pseudo-left in its astonishing anguish to produce a "Marxism of its own"—presumably to compete with the continental trends that cropped up around figures like Marcuse, Adorno, Sartre, Althusser, and so on—had to resort to none other than that repository of all the reactionary trends in European thinking in the early decades of the century—F. R. Leavis and *Scrutiny*.

As a prelude to the detailed examination of the relationship between the pseudo-left and Leavis, we point to the shameless tribute that it paid to him recently in the shape of the book we have already mentioned—*The Moment of Scrutiny* by Francis Mulhern. Published in 1979, it obviously found the time ripe for claiming openly and at length for the pseudo-left the heritage of the reactionary Leavis clique, which in the early sixties it only indirectly and somewhat bashfully acknowledged. Mincing no words, it comes out effusively with such praise as: "an ineffaceable image in the memory of national culture", "an irruption never ended into a cultural order perpetually vulnerable to its impact" and an unparalleled example of militant writing in 20th century British culture surpassing such works as Caudwell's *Studies in a Dying Culture*. The author singles out what he calls *Scrutiny*'s militant interventionist cultural practice which he regards as something that should be defended and honored by socialists. The study also affirms that the true continuators of *Scrutiny* and the real heirs to the Leavisite mantel are people like Raymond

Williams and Richard Hoggart whose books *Culture and Society* and *The Uses of Literacy* coincided with the rise of the New Left movement in the late fifties and early sixties, and concludes that *Scrutiny* has been the 'natural ally' of the left which must still discover 'something of its peerless militancy'.

By Way of George Orwell

George Orwell is a figure in the history of British cultural criticism who links the pre-war generation of reactionary modernists and the post-war "left" or "new left" generation of writers. He shares with both generations a basic antipathy to genuine socialism in questions of politics and a marked tendency towards chauvinism and elitism in questions of culture. Here we are not concerned with the openly political and openly reactionary last phase of Orwell, the period of *Animal Farm* and *Nineteen Eighty-Four*, although that was, in fact, the moment which summed up the whole tendency of the first generation and left its deep imprint on the whole endeavor of the second. Even in strictly literary/cultural terms, Orwell was the key continuator of the reactionary modernists and who are exemplified in our study by Eliot and Leavis, and the chief medium through whom this heritage was transmitted to the post-war cultural "New Left", the main aspects of which will be discussed in the next three chapters.

It was Orwell for example who was largely responsible, and at a very early date, for the myth of the great artists of the twenties—Eliot, Joyce, Lawrence, etc.—opposed to the "leftist propagandist" and, by implication, artistically compromised, writers of the thirties on the one hand and the traditionalist, parochial and, by implication, artistically stultified earlier generation of socialist writers like Shaw, Wells and others. This is clearly apparent in remarks like:

> One must admit that whether Lawrence's view of life is true or whether it is perverted: it is at least an advance on the Science worship of H.G. Wells or the shallow Fabian progressivism of writers like Bernard Shaw.[29]

As well as in the final conclusion of that comparison between the two generations which comes up with a strong endorsement of the reactionaries in spite—right in the midst of the Second World War—of their openly admitted and widely recognized fascist tendencies:

> Their revulsion from a shallow conception of progress drove them politically in the wrong direction, and it isn't an accident that Ezra Pound, for instance, is now shouting antisemitism on the Rome radio. But one must concede that their writings are

more grown-up, and have a wider scope, than what went immediately before them. They broke the cultural circle in which England had existed for something like a century. They re-established contact with Europe, and they brought back the sense of history and the possibility of tragedy. On that basis all subsequent English literature that matters two pence has rested, and the development that Eliot and the others started, back in the closing years of the last war, has not yet seen its course.[30]

In the same way the comparison between the right-wing writers of the twenties and the left-wing writers of the thirties in his famous essay, *Inside the Whale*, established the myth that the earlier generation was less political and hence better artists than the one which followed. The truth of the matter, of course, was that Eliot, Lawrence and Pound were no less political than the thirties generation. Only their politics, however much secretly approved of, was rather inappropriate in 1940. Therefore, since the question had become left politics or no politics at all—a reactionary would have to choose the latter course. And this is precisely where political and social apathy, which became such an important ingredient of the cultural ethos of the years following the Second World War, is raised and prophetically formulated in that same essay:

> On the whole the literary history of the 'thirties seems to justify the opinion that a writer does well to keep out of politics. For any writer who accepts or partially accepts the discipline of a political party is sooner or later faced with the alternative: toe the line or shut up.[31]

> The passive attitude will come back, and it will be more consciously passive than before. Progress and reaction have both turned out to be swindles. Seemingly there is nothing left but quietism . . . Give yourself over to the world-process, stop fighting against it or pretending that you control it; simply accept it, endure it, record it. That seems to be the formula that any sensitive novelist is now likely to adopt. A novel on more positive "constructive" lines, and not emotionally spurious, is at present very difficult to imagine.[32]

Of course the apolitical posture was no more than a posture.[33] Orwell was not opposed to all politics, only to socialist politics. Significantly his tirades against what he called the invasion of literature by politics, assumed an increasingly open reactionary character as the War ended and the Cold War ideology began to set in. Thus in his other important essay on the same theme, *Writers and Leviathan*, published for the first time in a journal edited by none other than Raymond Williams, one of the founders of the "New Left" in Britain, he came up with such blatant formulations as:

I am not, of course, suggesting that mental dishonesty is peculiar to socialists and left-wingers generally, or is commonest among them. It is merely that acceptance of *any* political discipline seems to be incompatible with literary integrity.[34]

Perhaps it is even a bad sign in a writer if he is not suspected of reactionary tendencies today, just as it was a bad sign if he was not suspected of Communist sympathies twenty years ago.[35]

Undoubtedly it is for this reason that Orwell was favorably received by *Scrutiny* and the leavisites, which was a rare honor for any contemporary writer. In an important review of *Inside the Whale* by Q.D. Leavis,[36] the wife and partner of the Guru, she described his works as 'responsible, adult and decent'. Not surprisingly, she singled out for praise the anti-socialist diatribe, *The Road to Wigan Pier*, and summed him up, in what was later to become a cliché of Orwell criticism, as an 'innately decent' writer. This decency, however, has a very special meaning for Mrs Leavis. It seems that in her eyes it is acquired if one displays and approves of "bourgeois morality" and if "he is disgusted" with what she refers to as the "inhumanity of the pro-Marxists." In the same manner, "the special kind of honesty" which she also finds in his works turns out to be a by-product of his attacks on the left-wing writers and critics of the thirties.

Finally, the other basic ingredient in Orwell's cultural position, namely, his chauvinism and social-chauvinism summed up in his famous statement that "no real revolutionary has ever been an internationalist" and destined later to infect deeply the "New Left" in Britain, is best displayed in his 1941 essay, *The Lion and the Unicorn*,[37] which is a rabidly rightist and prophetically McCarthyite attack on the intelligentsia, and by implication primarily the left-wing intelligentsia, for being severed from "the common culture of the country" and "ashamed of their own nationality."

· 2 ·

RAYMOND WILLIAMS: THE END OF THE LINE

Williams and Tradition

Raymond Williams is the direct continuator and apologist of the line of English literary and cultural criticism formed by Eliot, Lawrence and Leavis. His book *Culture and Society 1780–1950* is an attempt to resolve the internal contradictions between those three representative figures and to reconcile them to a previous romantic trend in English cultural criticism in order to construct a pseudo-tradition, much in the manner of those other pseudo traditions of his mentor, F.R. Leavis, to which he would become a legitimate successor. And a successor to that line, in spite of all the "leftist" terminology, he is. More than a successor, he is, in fact, also an apologist in that his account of the so-called tradition is a particularly false one, based as it is on selective quotations derived arbitrarily from certain works. He formulates a totally false idea, for example, of Lawrence, Eliot, Carlyle, and so on, by basing his discussion on one or two essays or books and quoting selectively from them. All that is glorified under the label of "close reading", of "confronting the text" and other such jargon of "practical criticism" and Leavisism.

For there is no doubt that Williams began his career as a Leavisite. His first work, *Reading and Criticism*, is a work of applied Leavisism with all the usual

terminology—"control", "centrality", "life", "organic", "experience," etc.—
associated with it. The book consists of the analysis of passages of verse and
prose all drawn from the works of writers in the approved Leavisite canon, like
George Eliot, Joseph Conrad, Yeats and Lawrence. In the preface to the book,
Williams openly acknowledges this debt. He writers: "Mr F.R. Leavis has been
largely responsible for the continuing development of critical analysis as an
educational discipline, and to his work, and that of *Scrutiny*, I am indebted".[1]
And in the text, he again refers admiringly to Leavis as a critic who, together
with I.A. Richards, "has done more to develop literary criticism and analysis
as an educational discipline than any other critic."[2] Later, Williams devoted
a whole section of his *Culture and Society* to Leavis, in which he described his
work as "a major achievement." This makes the essay doubly aggravating in
that Williams claims to reject the two basic Leavisite "concepts" of minority
culture and of the pre-industrial organic society. Finally, one of Williams's
early essays is titled openly "Our Debt to Dr Leavis" and begins with the abject
apology that "we must try to pay our debt to F.R. Leavis, whether or not he
will acknowledge us as debtors". He then continues to affirm that Leavis "is
the most interesting critic of his generation . . . and that his life's work is a
major contribution to our culture", and ends finally with the statement that
Leavis now is above whether one agrees or disagrees with him because he
is enshrined in that "Central English Tradition"—among the immortals, so
to speak—which ordinary readers may only serve and not think of repaying
because "such debts cannot be repaid."[3]

The metamorphosis of this reactionary Leavisite into the great Guru of
the New Left, and later into England's combined answer to Marcuse, Sartre,
Althusser and Lukacs is a reflection of the state of Britain's literary and cultural
intelligentsia. For a Guru, Williams has willy-nilly become, and everywhere
you read, there is effusive praise of his accomplishments and abject salutes
to his towering figure. E.P. Thompson has called him "the best man" of the
New Left and Perry Anderson has described *Culture and Society* and *The Long
Revolution* as "the major contribution to socialist thought in England since the
war."[4] *The New Left Review* publishing house has come out with a 400 odd page
book that consists of series of interviews with Williams on his life and work, in
the manner usually given only by "'Eminent figures", and if you add to that the
band of disciples like Terry Eagleton and the media scholars at Birmingham,
you have the picture complete. The English intellectual "Left" wants a father
figure, if for nothing, then at least it will keep those French philosophers and
German aestheticians at bay. England *must* have its own "national Marxism"

(the monstrous phrase coined by Perry Anderson); it seems to be a required boost for the collective ego of the "leftist" intelligentsia.

Culture and Society, the book which by all accounts launched Williams and, to a big extent, the New Left movement, is, in fact, an openly ideal-ist work. That much has been recognized by nearly everyone. There is no such tradition as the one described in it. Voices in the air and ghostly figures extending from Burke and Coleridge, to Orwell and Lawrence, do not link up into anything. Divorced from their social background they mean nothing. But, more importantly, *Culture and Society* is a deceitful, dishonest and, in the worst sense of the term, propagandistic work. As a false representation of nearly all of the figures discussed, it is, in one word, a fabrication. Such figures do not exist, not only as a tradition, but even in isolation. The work is not an accept-able history of ideas; it misrepresents and deliberately falsifies the material.

It is significant that, years later, when Williams was openly confronted with the charge of misrepresenting such key figures in his book as Burke, Carlyle, and Lawrence and of suppressing and falsifying their political positions, he could not but admit that "the honest thing to do and the right thing to do would have been to argue the case of each thinker fully and explicitly through, and say what was wrong with him."[5] He was also forced to say of what was once regarded as the Bible of the New Left in Britain, "Well, I respect *Culture and Society*, but it is not a book I could conceive myself writing now. I don't much know the person who wrote it. I read this book as I might read a book by someone else. It is a work most distant from me."[6]

At the time he wrote the book, Williams was certainly not distant from it. The work, in fact, is very much written in a spirit of self-aggrandizement in that, implicitly, it is the author who will continue the "Great Tradition" of the illustrious figures contained in it. Williams's procedure was mystifying, reactionary and chauvinistic. It had nothing to do with what the individual figures *really* did and said, whether they were romantics or realists, anarchists or conservatives, anti-capitalists or fascists, revolutionaries or reactionaries— what mattered was that they were Great English figures, and Williams was going to continue their work. Politically, Williams, of course, claimed to be a socialist. But his socialism was nothing but social-chauvinism, of the kind that "reconciles" conservatives with radicals, the Right with the Left, fascism with socialism, because in the end it is all in the *English* tradition.

Culture, the key word for Williams, is simply national culture. It is "the whole way of life" of the community, as defined by none other than T.S. Eliot. Therefore, any closer examination of this culture along class lines is not acceptable. The term used by Williams is not a sociological but an anthropological concept which acquires mystical and even racist connotations. If culture is not defined in class terms, and even in bourgeois sociological terms, then what are we left with except the nebulous, and ultimately irrational, concepts of blood-ties and race as in Lawrence, or soil and religion (and race) as in Eliot, etc., to the end of the reactionary, elitist and, ultimately, racist cultural "theorizing" of the modernist figures ? Williams's sole "innovation" is that he substitutes for the cultural elitism and open racism of these figures, his own community-culture, with a "leftist" tilt, that really amounts to no more than replacing open chauvinism with social-chauvinism, not a better if not a worse species.

Williams and Leavis

Williams came under the influence of Leavis at a very early and crucial stage in his development when he became a student of English literature at Cambridge University in the early forties. Although a member of the Socialist Club then, one of the first things he wrote was titled "Literature and the Cult of Sensibility", an attack on Bloomsbury, revealing, as he later admitted, that Leavis's criticism had obviously 'filtered through'.[7] Moreover it is very clear from his own account of those years that although politically on the left, he was in the affairs of culture and literature, very much on the Leavisite and modernist side. "We were pretty critical of socialist realism," Williams recounts, ". . . our interests were very much more in modernism. To take my own case, before I arrived at Cambridge I wanted to write like Shaw and Wells, whom I read at school . . . Then I changed very rapidly, with an incredible mixture of influences. But by the second year Joyce was without question the most important author for us. *Ulysses* and *Finnegans Wake*—which just appeared in 1939—were the texts we most admired, and we counterposed to socialist realism".[8] It is no surprise that the literary group to which he belonged in those years was contemptuously referred to as the 'Aesthetes'. What is significant (as we will show later in reference to his essay on Goldmann) is that in this divide between socialist realism and modernism, between Marxism and Leavisism, Williams *continued* to remain in the Leavisite, modernist camp *ever since*. Over the years and in various ways, he has affirmed his conviction in theoretical statements, as well as in studies of the novel and of drama, that the achievements of Leavis and of modernism were far superior, both in criticism and in literature, to those of Marxism and of socialist realism.

It seems also that Williams came under a strong psychological pressure at Cambridge because of the War and because of what he regarded as his academic incompetence. Looking back over those years, he says:

> You must remember that a hell of a lot of my self-image was devoted to the notion that I could handle academic work. It soon became clear that actually I could not . . . So it was a total mess of a situation. At the same time it did seem pretty irrelevant. Because you knew that you were going into the army in a few months and it seemed improbable that anything would eventuate from all this in any case. I have also got to say that it was a time of quite extraordinary personal and emotional disorder . . . I did not have anything as definable as a breakdown, but the situation was more than I could handle.[9]

This autobiographical passage is crucial because it was at this point, and under these disturbed psychological conditions, that Williams, although remaining nominally "on the Left", broke with Marxism and, more relevantly in this context, developed the conviction that in the field of literary and cultural studies Marxism was not academically "respectable". It is here that he became infected with the bourgeois academic virus—that long-established mechanism for keeping culture and art under the diseased domination of reactionaries.

When Williams came back to Cambridge at the end of the War, the break was complete. "The whole crisis had an important bearing on my attitude when I returned to academic work in 1945," he recollects, "People often ask me now why I didn't carry on then from the Marxist arguments of the thirties. The reason is that I felt they had led me into an impasse. I had become convinced that their answers did not meet the questions, and that I had got to be prepared to meet the professional objections. I was damned well going to do it properly this time."[10] Like any renegade, Williams tries to find objective "justifications" for his own subjective betrayal. "The student culture had altered," he describes Cambridge after the War. "There was a lot more religion about. There was also now a specific literary culture around Leavis, which was poles removed from what we had known in '41. There was really no longer a conscious left presence."[11]

It should come as no surprise then that the first project Williams embarked on in that period was to start, with two other Leavisites, a new reactionary, leavisite journal, *Politics and Letters*. In the four issues that ever came out of it, the journal was no more than a pale extension of *Scrutiny*.

Although Williams later claimed that its intention was to "unite radical left politics, with Leavisite literary criticism,"[12] its "leftism" in fact, did not go beyond carrying an advertisement for the communist *Modern Quarterly* on the inside back cover of only its first issue (an action that would indeed have been too radical for *Scrutiny*). Its rightism, however, was written all over—from vulgar attacks on Zhdanov to discussions of the usual array of names of reactionary journalism, Lawrence, Joyce, Yeats, etc. Far from being a leftist cultural liberation from *Scrutiny*; it was, in fact, dominated by *Scrutiny* and the *Scrutiny* ethos.

Its very first editorial is full of such Leavisite jargon as "greater awareness", "synthesis of human and material richness", "a more complete consciousness", etc. When we add to this, statements about "the most permanent and profound qualities of human experience (as seen, for example in the writings of Yeats and Lawrence)", and vulgar jibes at "English Marxism", the journal begins to look very much like a Cold War venture, and a pioneering venture at that, replete at that early date of 1947 with articles on *The Open Society* and discussions of The Truman Administration by W.W. Rostow.

The Leavisism of the journal became clearer in the combined second and third issues which opened with a quotation from Matthew Arnold to the effect that culture "does not try to teach down to the inferior classes; it does not try to win them over to this or that sect of its own, with ready judgments and watchwords." We are to understand that the *Politics* side of the journal has been defused, and the *Letters* side has predominated, particularly when we are also informed that the journal now incorporates its more literary companion *The Critic*, edited by the same board. The editorial also contained in its opening paragraph a re-statement of the old Leavisite circularity, a form of modernist aestheticism in fact, that literature cannot be explained in any terms except those of literature. It posed the question about what literature represents in society, and then it replied: "We cannot give an answer which would satisfy the social scientist, because the final statement cannot be given in terms of science. It is a literary statement." Finally, it went on to endorse the cult of D.H. Lawrence using the kind of vitalist terminology that is virtually indistinguishable from the language of F.R. Leavis:

> Perhaps we could put the question of what literature represents in another way. We can ask—what forms of human organization are compatible with our experience of litera-ture? Among modern writers it is D.H. Lawrence who has most to say on this question, whose writings are of central importance in the work which *Politics and Letters* will undertake on culture and environment . . . D.H. Lawrence realised in his work that deepest and innate *responsiveness* which is life, and defined the failure in responsibility, the absence or destruction of purpose, which is not life. He saw that responsibility for life in the present cannot be abandoned while planning for life in the future.

This sort of gibberish is quite meaningless except to indicate that the journal now had come under full Leavisite control. Significantly those two issues contained an article by Leavis himself as well as two major articles on Blake and Arnold by the Leavisites R.C. Churchill and Wolf Mankowitz.

Leavis's article is interesting in that it contains, first, his unqualified blessings of the journal—"I sympathize" he says, "with the aims I have associated with *Politics and Letters*"—and, secondly, it is a vulgar attack on Marxism in the person of Christopher Hill, in which he equates "adopting a historical attitude" toward literature with being subservient to Moscow, and, finally, it contains yet another restatement of his vitalist pseudo-philosophy of literature, the words of which are closely echoed in that passage from the editorial quoted above:

> To be seriously interested in literature is to be intensely and seriously interested in life. I myself am given to insisting that literary criticism is, or should be, a specific discipline of intelligence . . . literary criticism, conceived as a discipline, is to be defined rather in terms of a trained and cultivated ability to be relevant, etc.[13]

The fourth, and last, issue of the journal, by which time it had become almost a carbon copy of *Scrutiny*, is not worthy of much attention except for an article by George Orwell, which once again revealed the latent Cold War aspirations of the journal. It contained statements of the sort that require no comment, like: "It is merely that acceptance of *any* political discipline seems to be incompatible with literary integrity", and "perhaps it is even a bad sign in a writer if he is not suspected of reactionary tendencies".[14]

The whole project, then, of *Politics and Letters*, seems to have been started under the shadow of Leavis, as Williams himself later admitted. "We were all however," he recollected, "very anxious to see what Leavis would say about *us*. Because after all he never said anything good about a contemporary phenomenon. Mankowitz got him to write in *Politics and Letters*. What he said, with great tact, was that we would succeed if we lived up to a series of objectives that amounted to a description of *Scrutiny*."[15] And they did not succeed precisely for that reason. The magazine collapsed after four issues because *the other two editors*, and not Williams, abandoned Leavisism. "Collins retained most of Leavis's and Eliot's arguments," Williams explains, "but was increasingly centred on Freudian and related ideas. Mankowitz, on the other hand, broke right away from minority cultural positions."[16] Only Williams stuck it out as the adamant Leavisite. "For the next ten years I wrote in nearly complete isolation," he says, and the result was the cumbersome Leavisite applications and modifications in the areas of culture (*Culture and Society*), drama (*The drama from Ibsen to Eliot*) and the novel (*The English Novel from Dickens to Lawrence*), to which we shall turn next.

Drama and the Novel

In the Introduction to his book on the drama, Williams openly acknowledges his Leavisite critical method. Explaining:

> My criticism is, or is intended to be, literary criticism. It is literary criticism, also, which in its major part is of the kind based on demonstrated judgments from texts, rather than on historical survey, or generalized impressions of the kind, that is to say, which is known in England as practical criticism.[17]

Having established the well-known Leavisite dualism of "demonstrated judgments" versus "historical and generalized impression" (in reality a justification for the vulgar methodology of selective quoting in order to "push" a pre-determined reactionary ideology of "minority culture", "organic community", "life-affirmation", etc and to prevent the open discussion of historical and philosophic ideas in the literary cultural process), Williams goes on:

> Practical Criticism began, in the work of Eliot, Richards, Leavis, Empson, and Murray, mainly in relation to poetry. It has since been developed, notably by both F.R. and Q.D. Leavis, in relation to the novel. In the drama, apart from the work of Eliot on Elizabethan dramatists and of other critics on Shakespeare, the usefulness of practical criticism remains to be tested. This book, in addition, to its main objects, is intended, therefore, as a working experiment in the application of practical criticism methods to modern dramatic literature.[18]

What is more, Williams also affirms, in that very introduction, his allegiance to the reactionary core of Leavisism, and that is the concept of minority culture. "Very powerful arguments can be advanced in support of the idea that a fully serious drama is impossible in a society where there is no common system of belief."[19] He begins with the familiar theme, and then continues "in an age of widespread community of individual belief, the conventions of this process (the process of drama writing) are already easier to establish, and full communication is more likely. But at all times, the community between artist and audience which seems to matter is the *community of sensibility* . . . There is no such common sensibility today. The pressure of a mechanical environment has dictated mechanical ways of thought, feelings and conjunction, which artists, and a few of like temper, reject only by conscious resistance and great labour. That is why all serious literature, in our own period, tends to become minority literature (although the minority is capable of extension and in my view has no social correlative). But within that minority, serious literature, even serious drama, is in fact possible: Mr Eliot's plays are not the only evidence," and he concludes, "it is not the lack of common beliefs in society which restricts his [the artist's] communication. It is rather the lack of certain qualities of living, certain capacities for experience. Thus drama at the present time, if it is to be serious in the full traditional sense, is inevitably minority drama."[20] This is a passage that basically requires no comment: The switch from the Eliotic "community of belief" to the Leavisite "community of sensibility", the obligatory respect for Mr Eliot's dramatic achievement, the Laurentian thirst for certain qualities of living and certain capacities for experience and, to tie it all together, the final affirmation of the inevitably minority drama—all speak too clearly for themselves.

Williams's book on the novel, although on appearance anti-Leavisite in that it gives importance to novelists, like Dickens and Hardy, who are not given a place in Leavis's so-called Great Tradition, is still a very Leavisite work both in methodology and in conceptual framework. Take for example, statements like:

> It is still widely believed that the traditional culture of the English people was broken and disintegrated by the Industrial Revolution. What then emerged, it is said, was on the one hand a debased synthetic commercial culture—the world of the newspapers and popular entertainment; on the other hand an increasingly threatened minority culture—an educated tradition within which the finest literature and thought of the time sought to maintain and extend itself and keep its connections, its continuities, with the best work of the past. Each of these descriptions seems to me partially true. . .[21]

> It is now conventional in critical accounts of the English novel to go on from George Eliot to Henry James. There is of course a real relation there . . . But first I am interested in emphasising a more central English tradition: from George Eliot to Hardy and then on to Lawrence, which is a very clear and in my view decisive sequence.[22]

This can only be described as slightly modified Leavisism. What would have been expected from the editor of the May Day Manifesto of 1968, and of the Guru of the New Left which Williams by 1970 had become, was not a qualified approval of reactionary Leavisite dogma about the "disintegration of traditional culture" and the concern for the so-called "threatened minority culture", but for a radical break from it. Similarly, replacing James by Hardy or putting Dickens in the center rather than on the periphery of the so-called "central English tradition" is no substitute for the genuinely revolutionary step of repudiating the whole Leavisite endeavor of line-drawing and tradition-mapping, and for exposing it as reactionary, idealist and chauvinistic. Williams, however, is far from doing any such thing. In this book, as in the earlier work on drama, as well as in *Culture and Society*, which we discussed in the beginning of this chapter, he is back at the old methodology of so-called practical criticism—i.e. quoting selected passages to "prove" pre-conceived notions about the writer and the tradition, without actually arguing out those assumptions explicitly. This is practical criticism indeed—it is practical for proving whatever you want it to prove. Demagogic criticism would be a far more suitable name for it.

From Leavis to Goldmann?

Perhaps the best summation of Williams's relationship to Leavis and to *Scrutiny* is his 1971 essay, "Literature and Sociology—in the Memory of Lucien Goldmann",[23] which is more illuminating about Williams himself, and particularly his relationship to Leavis, than it is about Goldmann. We will not go into that essay in detail, we merely wish to show that here again Williams re-affirms his allegiance to Leavis and implicitly to the "central English tradition" within a theoretical context and at a farther historical distance, although ostensibly the essay is about how he has moved *away* from all that, into the European world of Goldmann, Lukacs, and Benjamin, et al. This allegiance here comes out not in terms of acknowledgement of debt or application of ideas as in the earlier phase of Williams, nor even in the mythologizing of the Tradition as in the *Culture and Society* phase, but in the historical stance which Williams now assumes and in which his verdict is so blatantly in favor of *Scrutiny* and the Leavisites: "In the 1930's this kind of diagnosis (the Leavisite school of criticism) overlapped, or seemed to overlap, with other radical interpretations, and especially, perhaps with the Marxist interpretation of the effects of capitalism. Yet almost at once there was a fundamental hostility between these two groups, a critical engagement between *Scrutiny* and the English Marxists, which we can have little doubt, looking back, *Scrutiny* won." First of all, the placement of *Scrutiny*'s proto-fascist and blatantly reactionary ideology together with Marxism under the same label of "radical" is indication enough of where Williams really stands, but to add to it that *Scrutiny* won the battle is really adding insult to injury. And what does "winning" mean in this case?

Reading further on, one finds out the answer to that question. Williams does not refer to a temporary defeat or to an unfavorable balance of forces, but to a genuine, final and well-deserved victory. He affirms that the *Scrutiny* critics won because they were 'much closer to literature' and, more fundamentally, because they did not resort to such useless terms as 'base and superstructure' and did not fall into the trap of so-called economic reductionism. They alone could give "an account of art which in its closeness and intensity at all corresponded to the real human dimension in which art works are made and valued". So much then for all the reactionary poison that permeated the pages of *Scrutiny*. All that is forgotten, if it were ever recognised. Looking back now, Williams gives the final historical verdict. And where is that published? In none other than that foremost intellectual "leftist" journal—the *New Left Review*. Williams even has the audacity to replace what he calls the 'formula of base and superstructure' with what he innovates as 'the more active idea of a field of mutually if also unevenly determining forces' (whatever that means). What Williams does in this essay is not to pay tribute to Goldmann nor to present new ways in literary and cultural criticism (the so-called 'structures of feeling' and the 'field of mutually determining forces' and other such jargon which even his New Left cohorts do not take seriously), but to add to the triumph of the Leavisite interpretation of English cultural history which he affirmed in works like *Culture and Society*, the allegation of the continuing triumph of Leavisism in the twentieth century. Thus, beneath the pseudo-socialist mask, and the European openness to Goldmann, Lukacs, and Sartre, etc., there lurks the same English chauvinist Leavisite.

Williams and Orwell

The most blatant evidence of Williams's continuing adherence to the pseudo tradition constructed in *Culture and Society*, and specifically to the reactionary 20th century segment of it, is the full-length book he wrote, *thirteen years later,* about George Orwell.[24] That such a book should have been written at all is astounding. Here we have the man said to be more than anyone else responsible for rejuvenating socialist culture in Britain, the cultural Guru of the New Left, a figure celebrated in the pages of New *Left Review* as the Grand Thinker of the "left" intelligentsia in Britain, nothing less, in fact, than Britain's com-pound answer to such continentals as Lukacs, Marcuse and Althusser, writing a book about none other than the degenerate, sado-masochistic misanthrope and anti-democratic, anti-socialist Cold War hack—George Orwell. The sur-prise, however, should only be momentary for those who see. Williams and the pseudo-left *could only* be the political heirs of George Orwell, just as cultur-ally they were the followers of Lawrence and Leavis. As the historically clos-est major figure discussed in *Culture and Society*, Orwell, in fact, represented the most suitable combination of pseudo-socialism and Trotskyism covering a core of reactionary and chauvinistic ideas. More than anyone else, he was the immediate ancestor of the pseudo-left. Williams continued to refer to Lawrence and Leavis in various articles, but of all the figures in *Culture and Society*, only Orwell received the privilege of a full-length book.

Chauvinism is the first link that binds Orwell and Williams firmly from the start, and Williams from the very opening chapter establishes this connec-tion. "He creates the sense of an England of basic ordinariness and decency, a 'real England',"[25] says Williams endorsing the trite, jingoistic cliché of Orwell criticism. But typically enough, he goes on to make the preposterously distort-ing statement that "Orwell's great influence since the 1940's owes as much to this powerful image as to "any other single achievement,"[26] as if Orwell, the rabid anti-democrat, anti-humanist, and anti-socialist Cold War propagandist had never existed, and all that he represented was a decent, gentle, patriotic English writer. This is not just going against the evidence; it is blatant falsi-fication of the crudest kind. Orwell, precisely since the 1940's was no longer simply a provincial writer of the English theme, he was *the* major reactionary, imperialist cultural mouthpiece, and his only "great" achievement was the service of the ruling Cold War ideology of that epoch. William's judgment is not just a minor distortion—it is a big lie. Furthermore, it is condemned by its own very words. The fig-leaf of patriotism, by which he tries to cover up the ugly features of Orwell's writing, turns out to be no more than the despised Union Jack of British imperialism. "His further emphasis on the gentleness and mildness of much ordinary English life," Williams continues, "on these qualities being positive achievements in a world of killing and anger, is again reasonable." Reasonable indeed. In this very juxtaposition of the gentle and mild 'ordinary English life' against the 'world of killing and anger', the true colors of Williams, the imperialist apologist masquerading as a socialist, are fully revealed. For it should be elementary to any true socialist that Britain in the forties and fifties, as the chief, or at least one of the chief, imperialist powers, was directly responsible for most of the 'killing and anger' in the world, that the so-called 'gentleness and mildness' of English life was *built* upon the ruthless exploitation and murderous suppression of the hundreds of millions of the world's population.

Having established Orwell's "Englishness", as befits the chauvinistic Leavisite, Williams proceeds in exactly the manner followed in *Culture and Society* with regard to Lawrence, to whitewash Orwell, to smooth over the sharp edges, so that, in the end, we come up with an Orwell that is just as unbelievable as the leftist, liberal-humanist Lawrence. First of all, it is amazing dishonesty for any writer on Orwell, and even more so for a self-proclaimed socialist writer, to cover up for Orwell's sickening invective against socialism in the second half of *The Road to Wigan Pier*, as well as his simply obtuse and irrational attacks on such movements as feminism, pacifism and birth control. Reading the pages Williams devotes to that work (pages 12, 13 and 50 to 54) one gets the impression that, in fact, it was Orwell who was in the right and the socialist movement which was in the wrong. This is the matter-of-fact approach adopted by Williams: "Repeating his opposition to imperialism and the class system," says Williams affirming this so-called 'opposition' as an established fact drawn from Orwell's earlier books, "he now adds a commitment to socialist definitions of freedom and equality while at the same time attacking most forms of the organised socialist movement and especially various kinds of English middle-class socialists."[27]

There you have it—in a word, Orwell's sham socialism and real anti-socialism, recognized by readers of the book from the start,[28] must be accepted as genuine, against the positions of the real socialists of the time. Williams even has the audacity—for a self-proclaimed socialist and a founder of the New Left—to dismiss the Foreword to the book written by Victor Gallancz[29] as representative of the Left Book Club which commissioned the book, in which he dissociated the Club from Orwell's anti-socialist slanders and exposed them as an expression of his bourgeois background and mentality—as a mere "cautionary note" without any further ado. In the same dishonest manner, Williams literally turns the matter on its head when he refers to Orwell's activities in Spain—where, in fact, he went to put the anti-socialism he expressed in *The Road to Wigan Pier* into practice—as a time that "sharpened" his outlook into "a positive position" and turned him, believe it or not, according to Williams, into "a revolutionary socialist".

Here the great critic's methodology, his big lie tactic, consists of one simple operation—to paint the black white and the white black. In the same way, he more than implies that that commonly recognized (by critics of all kinds of views) anti-socialist diatribe, *Nineteen Eighty-Four* is, in fact, not anti-socialist, but anti-fascist.[30]

With *Animal Farm*, Williams follows the on-the one-hand and on-the other-hand kind of approach which, under the guise of a judicious balancing act, makes a strong endorsement of that weak anti-socialist fable which has been recognized as such even by the reactionary critics. Thus, we are told that the book is "a work of simplification in both the good and the bad senses," that it has "the precision of political aim" which is contradicted by "the search for simplicity and generality"[31] and, finally, that judgments of the work must go beyond easy exploitation" and "equally easy rejection"[32]. All of this, however, is no more than an act, a simulation of so-called "critical analysis" and "profound response". It is not even the evasive tactic, which it at first appears to be, of refusing to say whether the book is "good" or "bad", whether it should be "exploited" or "rejected". For, in fact, Williams soon sinks into most abject praise of the book, which surpasses even the comments of the older, Cold War critics[(33)]. Orwell, we are told, is able "to generate an immediate and practical humanity" out of a "despairing base", that he reveals "an assured and active and laughing intelligence" manifested in "the penetration and exposure of the experience of defeat, that he is "able to release an exceptionally strong and pure prose", etc. His final verdict lapses so revealingly into the old Leavisite jargon—"liberating intelligence", "connects and informs", "radical energy", etc.—always a sure and recognizable sign of literary cretinism that it deserves a long citation:

> In many places through *Animal Farm* this strong and liberating intelligence transforms a bitter perception into an active and stimulating critique. Beyond the details of the local analogy, and paradoxically beyond the more fundamental despair, this lively awareness connects and informs . . . In its small scale and within its limited terms, *Animal Farm* has a radical energy which goes far beyond its occasion and has its own kind of permanence.[34]

Similarly, with *Nineteen Eighty-Four*, though here Williams tones down his enthusiasm a bit, we are told that the novel is divided between 'isolated feelings' and 'a more liberating consciousness.' On the one hand, it is marred by propagandistic misrepresentation and anti-humanism (cautiously implied by Williams), on the other hand (and here Williams is much more explicit) 'its central perception' is 'powerful', as an enemy of dictatorship Orwell is 'very close and alive' and 'his vision of power politics is also close and convincing.'[35]

After all this Williams's summation and concluding remarks on Orwell
come as no surprise. He begins again, however, in his familiar double-dealing
manner by posing the pseudo-problem of how Orwell's "inheritance" could be
fought over by both the Right and the Left, of how he could be regarded as
both a socialist and a reactionary at the same time. It is a pseudo-problem simply because Orwell was *never* a real socialist and the Left that fights over him
can be nothing but sham. There are no paradoxes and contradictory tendencies of the kind Williams ascribes to Orwell, who was nothing but a pseudo-
socialist in the early thirties but very quickly turned into the rabid reactionary
that he became known as till the day he died. That, in fact, is all there is to it.

The final chapter in the book is revealing not for what it tells about
Orwell, but for what it tells about Williams himself. For here we are given the
open and frank admission that the New Left in its early years, i.e. the years in
which Williams played a prominent part, regarded itself as follower of Orwell
and worshipped him as an ancestor. Here we have the astounding verdict
that those so-called radicals actually thought, in connection with *The Road to
Wigan Pier*, that "Orwell, unlike other socialists, understood English life—its
pace, its tolerance its distrust of abstractions and of any theory pushed to
extremes."[36] What this means is simply that the so-called socialists or radicals
of the fifties of the Williams type, actually sided with Orwell in his reactionary attacks on the socialists of the thirties. No wonder then that when those
"radicals" turned into a political movement—the New Left—they regarded
themselves as Orwell's continuators.

Williams explains:

> We could call these views and mood Orwell's inheritance. But it is then all the more
> remarkable that the generation for whom Suez, Hungary, and the Bomb were sig-
> nals for the renewal of political action looked to him with respect; a generation that
> believed not only in a new socialist movement, but one based on disturbance, on the
> politics of the street and the localities. This New Left respected Orwell directly, and
> especially in its early years.[37]

After this Williams, in the final pages of the book, sinks into the most
abject laudatory mood, surpassing even the rabid Cold War admirers of Orwell.
"He was the writer," we are told, "who put himself out, who kept going and
taking part, and who learned to write as a function of this very precise explo-
ration."[38] In the very last paragraph, Williams finally sinks on his knees in
reverence. "We are never likely to reach a time," he concludes "when we can
do without his frankness, his energy, his willingness to join in."[39]

The Last Phase

On the surface it appears that Williams's work after his book on Orwell took a new direction. In the seventies—so the argument often heard in New Left circles goes—he opened up to so-called "Western Marxism" and came under its influence. He went, as the title supplied by *New Left Review* to one of his later essays indicated, *from* Leavis *to* Goldmann. For him now Drama since Ibsen no longer stopped with Eliot; it extended all the way to Brecht. We see more and more frequently essays by Williams on such continentals as Timpanaro, Goldmann, Bahro and Solzhenitsyn. Furthermore, in the series of interviews given to the *New Left Review* at the end of the decade, Williams implicitly made an extended self-criticism of his early Leavisism and openly repudiated what may be called his *Culture and Society* phase.

In the introduction to *Marxism and Literature* (1978), which together with *The Country and The City* (1973) are his two major books of this period, Williams explains the background to his new development—how 'exceptionally isolated' he was in the forties and fifties, how he had to find his own way through writing *Culture and Society* making his way, as it were, through the Scylla and the Charybdis of Leavisism and Marxism, how he came into contact in the New Left period with Lukacs and Brecht, and, finally, in the late sixties and seventies, how he discovered the works of Goldmann, Althusser the later Lukacs and the later Sartre, Benjamin and Gramsci. With this he was finally liberated from his allergy to Marxism inculcated in him, not through any fault of his of course, but as a consequence of the debasement of Marxism in the thirties by that all-purpose *bete-noire* of the pseudo-leftist British intellectual—Stalinism. Because it creates such a false impression, this account can only be termed dishonest, and is, in fact, quite at variance with the NLR interviews referred to earlier. First of all, Williams was not 'isolated' through any adverse external circumstances or any personal independence of mind as is implied here. The latter is, in fact, a myth first propagated by E.P. Thompson in his review of Williams's *The Long Revolution* (to be discussed in the next chapter) which was the beginning of the Williams cult in the New Left circles. Williams was 'isolated' through his own conscious and deliberate decision to break with Marxism which, in those Cambridge days, never went very deep into him and was always overpowered by a stronger tendency toward aestheticism. Unlike hundreds of his generation he *chose* the "independent" path. Furthermore, his "isolation" was by no means absolute. In fact, he was very dependent on Leavisism. As we have seen his break with Marxism coincided with his conversion to vulgar bourgeois academism and with his openly Leavisite literary activities through the initiation of the journal *Politics and Letters*. Throughout the late forties and early fifites, he remained on that path producing work like *Reading and Criticism*, *Drama from Ibsen to Eliot* and *Culture and Society*, all heavily influenced by Leavis.

Therefore, the Marxism which Williams so contemptuously dismissed in that chapter on "Marxism and Culture" in *Culture and Society* was not just the Marxism of the thirties, it was Marxism *tout court*. It is a base falsification to say that he was aware of other kinds of more "original" Marxism way back in the forties—to which the rejected variety was implicitly contrasted. The early New Left, as we will see in the next chapter, which came to regard *Culture and Society* as its key text was, in fact, based on the rejection of Marxism and its replacement by what was called socialist humanism. Williams's latter-day opening-up to the influence of "Western Marxism", i.e. to the pseudo-Marxist works of Lukacs, Althusser, Goldmann, etc., must then be regarded as a continuation of his earlier and basically anti-Marxist position. His work, like that of the Western pseudo-Marxists he is now so receptive to, is not a development or a creative application of the Marxist ideology and the Marxist world outlook; it is diametrically opposed to them. The book, furthermore, is even more disappointing than those of the continental pseudo-Marxists, consisting as it does of the abstract classification of pseudo concepts like 'homology', 'mediation', 'hegemony', etc., derived from those writers plus a set of new coinage of his own like the notorious 'structures of feeling' and the pseudo-discipline of 'cultural materialism'.

Williams's earlier work, *The Country and the City*, is even more obviously a new direction but with a false start. Part of the essential purpose of the book seems to be to repudiate the reactionary idealization of pre-industrial society *a la* Eliot and Leavis. The critical methodology of the book also sharply departs from the 'close reading' of 'practical criticism', regards literature at a distance and against a concrete historical background. This undoubtedly is a step forward, however belated. As usual with Williams, however, this also lands him into newer fallacies particularly in connection with Marxism. It seems that Williams could never get over a basic inability to understand key Marxist concepts and a recurring tendency to compensate for that by the urge to "modify" and to "develop" upon what he implicitly held to be faults and inadequacies in Marxism. Thus, we get in *The Country and the City*, the book where Williams more militantly confronts his Leavisite Eliotic heritage than anywhere else, vulgar, contemptuous references to the Marxist notion of progress and to the

Marxist dialectic. It seems that for Williams every step forward just has to be accompanied by a step backward. His long-awaited liberation from the reactionary English literary-cultural tradition, which here seems real enough, is coupled with a vulgar and facile dismissal of the historical experience of socialism.

Still, *The Country and the City* is a major advance for at least two reasons. First, alone among Williams's rather substantial *oeuvre* it contains explicit indications that he is at least aware of the existence of literatures and cultures outside Europe. His pertinent references to Asian and African writing, to works by Yashar Kemal, Narayan, Achebe and others is a sign of greater awareness particularly for one brought up and educated in the reactionary English school of literary-cultural criticism. Secondly, it contains in the last two chapters the beginning of an understanding that imperialism stands behind the major contradictions of the world today. Although it is never spelled out, one hopes that Williams has moved towards comprehending the basic idea that the collapse of the imperialist system is the essential prerequisite for any socialist transformation, for any abolition of the division between the town and the countryside which he accurately conceives as an ultimate goal. Now these two observations are indeed elementary enough, yet it is a reflection more of the backwardness of the English tradition than of Williams himself, that such an acknowledgement of the role of imperialism and of the contribution of non-European peoples, seems like such a big step forward.

Unfortunately, this promising development is marred, as we said earlier by his almost obstinate refusal to learn from Marxism, as can be seen in a remark like: "Look at socialism or communism: historically the enemies of capitalism, but in detail and often in principle, in matters of the country and the city, continuing and even intensifying some of the same fundamental processes".[40] And we are back to square one. This long-exposed gimmick of equating capitalism and socialism, with its implicit recommendation of some kind of "third way", is merely self-defeating. More significantly, it is, for Williams, yet another form of rationalizing and justifying the earlier rejection of Marxism and the simultaneous adherence to a reactionary English literary and cultural trend. Williams recalls once more what seems to have been a traumatic experience:

> I can now look back a generation, to the immediate postwar years, and remember my feeling that except for certain simple kinds of idealising retrospect there was no main current of thought in the world which had not been incorporated within the fundamental forms of the capitalist and imperialist system. Orthodox communism and orthodox social-democracy—its traditional opponents—indeed showed many

features of this system in their most powerful forms, all the more dangerously because they had been fused with continuing aspirations to social liberation and development. But to feel this was to be pressed back towards the extreme subjectivism and fatalism which then, and for a generation, dominated our thought. Many descriptions of our current crisis were and still are cast within these subjectivist and fatalist forms.[41]

Now the comment that obviously needs to be made here is that the correctly diagnosed subjectivism and fatalism can be overcome not by equating communism with capitalism, and thus mystifying and rationalizing the reactionary Leavisism and the break with Marxism of those years, but to openly admit those aberrations as the only way to overcome them and move forward from there. Only this can put an end to the dishonest self-delusion that all those compromises with Leavis, with Orwell, with the whole reactionary cultural ethos, with the Cold War ideology, were due to this exceptionally heightened awareness (an unbelievably unique phenomena for the 1940's) of the inadequacies of the then current socialism. This, of course, is the well-known process of self-criticism which seems that Williams had been moving towards, unfortunately all too slowly in the seventies, and it might well have been too late for it ever to be performed.

· 3 ·

E.P. THOMPSON AND PERRY ANDERSON: A DEBATE

Introduction

The beginning of what may be called the cult of Raymond Williams can be traced back to the two-part review of *The Long Revolution* by E.P. Thompson in *New Left Review*. Written in 1961, the article is the initiation of a process that culminated two decades later in the series of interviews with Williams—in the manner one usually sees given by "eminent" European thinkers, like a Sartre or a Lukacs—produced in a big volume under the title of *Politics and Letters* by the NLR's own publishing house.

Thompson has no reservations about Williams and his work. "So far we can speak of a New Left," he declares, "he is our best man." His work is "very important indeed," we are told, and it can be ignored by critics, educational theorists, sociologists *and* political theorists only at their peril. "Even a brief passage of his writing," Thompson gets carried away, "[has] a sense of stubborn, unfashionable integrity, a combination of distinction and force."

Paradoxically, the essay is a critique, and a very forceful and persuasive critique, of the method, the conceptual framework, as well as the supposed achievement of the works of Raymond Williams. Yet, the persistent and incredible praise continues unabated. At one place Williams is even accredited with having "at many points a more constructive insight into the possibilities of socialism in this country than anyone living." Toward the end of the essay, he is again described as "a thinker of such force and principle that he has made it inevitable that [his] arguments be taken up." The New Left, we are told, will move forward and gain in intellectual coherence only if it comes to terms with his works.

Any reader who is perplexed, as he must be, by the terms of such an adulation, particularly in the light of the criticism which the rest of the essay contains, will have to attribute it to strictly subjective motivation. Indeed, there is ample evidence that the essay is written in the spirit of image-making and cult-building, of raising, for special purposes, a figure beyond what is warranted by his actual accomplishments. In this case, the purpose is to build up a "leftist" movement that is badly in need of a father figure. Williams, *as a person*, is described heroically as one who stood his ground while others abandoned the field. In one crucial passage, he is pointed out as literally *the only one* who did not succumb to reaction in the immediate post-war years. Unbelievably, we are told that "Raymond Williams is one of the very few intellectuals in this country who was not broken in some degree during that decade; and who maintained his independence from the attractive poles of cold war ideology." The truth of the matter, of course, is that Williams was no such hero, and that he was as compromised to reactionary ideology as anyone Thompson may have been thinking of. For this we shall now give some evidence from Thompson's own essay, instead of going over the ground already covered in our previous discussion of Williams and of his deep links, in outlook and methodology, to the Eliot-Lawrence-Leavis heritage.

To begin, this is how Thompson singles out the idealist method of *Culture and Society* and links it directly to the reactionary concept of tradition as used by Eliot:

> At times in *Culture and Society*, I felt that I was being offered a procession of disembodied voices—Burke, Carlyle, Mill, Arnold—their meanings wrested out of their whole social context . . . the whole transmitted through a disinterested spiritual medium. I sometimes imagine this medium (and it is the church-going solemnity of the procession which provokes me to irreverence) as an elderly gentlewoman and near relative of Mr. Eliot, so distinguished as to have become an institution: The Tradition.[1]

What Thompson finds objectionable is that Williams should regard his book as an answer to Eliot who, in Williams' words, had "raised questions which those who differ from him politically must answer, or else retire from the field." Thompson, on the other hand, finds Eliot's *Notes towards the Definition of Culture* 'a mediocre book', and is even more aggravated by the fact that it is not only 'that tone and those mannerisms of style which are derived from Eliot' but that '*it is also that Williams has accepted to some degree his opponent's way of seeing the problem.*' Here I think Thompson puts his finger on it. Of course, Eliot's book is more than just 'mediocre'—it is a pernicious product of a reactionary mind. But, at least one thing is recognized, and that is the fact that Williams has not escaped its influence. Further on, Thompson again rightly points to the so-called definition of culture as 'a whole way of life' which undermines the socialist nature of William's endeavor by enslaving him to this Eliotic 'way of seeing the problem'. This 'whole way of life' is suspect for several reasons, Thompson correctly observes. "It derives from Eliot, and in its first assertion is associated with religion." And, "despite the qualification," Thompson concludes, "Eliot's ghost haunts Mr Williams—and other NLR writers—whenever they mention 'the whole way of life'." Thompson, however, still does not take the issue seriously enough and leaves it as referring to something vague and harmless like 'style of life'. The idea of culture as 'a whole way of life' when carefully examined, however, can only be either a harking back to a romantic, reactionary concept of community as opposed to a class-based social formation, or a variation upon the modern fascistic notion of community based on soil, or blood, or religion, or race or whatever. In either case, it is meant to oppose the socialist concept of class culture which, presumably, Thompson and his NLR friends were trying to re-activate.

In spite of this qualification, Thompson is to be commended for pinpointing the key *conceptual* weakness of Williams' work. The abstractness of method and the 'impersonal construction' of style, which again he attributes to the influence of Eliot, and he might have added Leavis, are found to be a reflection and an expression of the inadequacy of the basic ideas upon which the whole endeavor is founded—e. g. concepts like "structures of feeling", "growth" of "new patterns" and the recurring trinity of "culture", "tradition" and "life".

The Debate

The third figure who entered this debate on English culture was Perry Anderson, the new editor of *New Left Review*. His 1965 essay, "Origins of the Present Crisis", initiated a new phase in which over the period of several years Thompson and Williams again participated.

The first striking thing about Anderson's essay is how it begins, almost as if in a conspiracy of adulation, with the obligatory reference to Raymond Williams, "whose *Culture and Society* and *The Long Revolution*", we are dutifully informed, "undoubtedly represent the major contribution to socialist thought in England since the war"[2]. In fact, the main aim of the essay, it turns out, is to fill in the historical dimension to what it calls the 'ethical' criticism of British society performed by Williams. So here we have another instance of the 'great Tradition' marching on. Just as Williams had to have the right ancestors—Arnold, Eliot, Lawrence, etc.—whose work he would carry forward, so is Anderson now continuing the next leg of the cultural relay race. It is ironic how Anderson and the New Left that he represents are afflicted by the very traditionalism and ancestor-worship which he claims, in this very essay, to be one of the constant sicknesses of British culture.

Anderson's essay is divided into two parts—one historical, the other cultural. The first part, which claims to give a 'totalizing' history of modern British society, is really an idealistic, one-sided pseudo-history from the 17th to the 20th century. Particular historical events are not anchored to a socio-economic basis, but are abstracted into historical concepts to fit an already pre-determined and one-sided model. Furthermore, it follows a superficial, comparativist methodology which explains a historical phenomenon not in terms of the internal factors that determine its nature, but in comparison to *other*, external phenomena. Thus, we are told that England had 'the most mediated, and least pure bourgeois revolution of any major European country' or that 'alone of all major European nations, England emerged undefeated and unoccupied from Two World Wars,' etc. What statements of this kind do is merely to *point* to the specificity English conditions without even attempting to make an analysis of the socio-historical basis of those conditions.

The cultural section of the essay, like its first part, is equally ambitious, and equally false and idealist. Again, ideologies and cultural "hegemonies" are not linked to socio-historical epochs, but are abstracted from a pre-conceived model. Traditionalism and empiricism, for example, are singled out as the permanent ruling class ideologies in Britain. This is sheer one-sidedness for clearly these are only *elements* in the ruling ideology which encompassed various other trends. What is more damnable in such a method, is that by one-sidedly singling out certain aspects of ruling class ideology, it glosses over the real socio-economic base from which it springs and to which it must owe its characterization. Thus, the ruling ideology in Britain from the 1880's onward can only be described as imperialism. All other trends, e.g. conservatism, jingoism, liberalism, protectionism, chauvinism, pseudo-socialism, etc, must be seen as aspects of it. Similarly, the ruling ideology in pre-imperialist Britain was industrial capitalism. Utilitarianism, bourgeois political economy, mechanical materialism, and so on, could only arise *within* it, i.e. they were developed by the industrial bourgeoisie and in the service of its system.

The whole discussion of the British working class is also plagued by the same idealist bend, this time refined by the abuse of inadequate terms like hegemonism and corporatism borrowed from Gramsci. Anderson fails in his analysis of working class reformism in Britain because he refuses to see the socio-economic basis of that reformism in the imperialist super-profits that have led to the creation of the labor-aristocratic class.

To point out all the faults and inaccuracies of Anderson's essay takes us outside our theme of cultural criticism. For our purposes it is enough to empha-size that our third figure—later to become another Guru of the New Left—has entered the debate with the same adulation of Williams and the Tradition, in an essay that is ostensibly a critique of British ruling class ideology and a 'total-izing history of British society' that claims to reveal where it all went wrong. For it is clear that with this essay Anderson is already speaking in a Guru-like tone. He has the answer to it all. And the answer is near-total rejection of British history and British culture (with the exception of Williams and the Tradition) and its replacement by a continental—mainly French and German with some Italian—recipe. And here begins the two-decade endeavor of *New Left Review* of propagating the works of so-called Western Marxism ranging from Sartre to Lukacs, to Marcuse, to Adorno, to Benjamin, etc. Over a hun-dred or more copies of the NLR these writers were "sold" to the students and teachers of British universities, and advertised in the most glowing terms. And now, after this exhausting marathon, where more than enough has been said, and made and sold, Mr. Anderson comes up with his latest book, *Considerations on Western Marxism*, in which he provides us with another devastating cri-tique, revealing all the faults and failures of the very merchandise he has been selling all those years. And so it all goes on, and the NLR publishing house comes out with yet another "required" book on the university reading lists.

But going back now to the debate of the mid-sixties, Anderson's essay was quickly answered by Thompson (whom he, significantly, had replaced as the editor of NLR) in a perceptive essay titled "The Peculiarities of the English", which was published in *The Socialist Register* that same year. Thompson has a good time tearing Anderson's "theories" to pieces, and he makes a good job of it. The reader who is interested in watching a slow-motion collapse of the flimsy structure of Anderson's argument should enjoy it. The essay is also important for the light it throws on the formation of the New Left, and the personal squabbles involved in it as revealed by its opening paragraph:

> Early in 1962, when the affairs of the *New Left Review* were in some confusion, the New Left Board invited an able contributor, Perry Anderson, to take over the editorship. We found (as we had hoped) in Comrade Anderson the decision and the intellectual coherence necessary to ensure the review's continuance. More than that, we discovered that we had appointed a rentable Dr. Beeching of the socialist intelligentsia. All the uneconomic branch lines and socio-cultural sidings of the New Left which were, in any case, carrying less and less traffic, were abruptly closed down. The main lines of the review underwent an equally ruthless modernization. Old Left steam-engines were swept off the tracks; wayside halts ("Commitment", "What Next for CND?," "Women in Love") were boarded up; and the lines were electrified for the speedy traffic from the Marxistentialist Left Bank. In less than a year, the founders of the review discovered, to their chagrin, that the Board lived on a branch-line which, after rigorous intellectual costing, had been found uneconomic. Finding ourselves redundant we submitted to dissolution.[3]

So this is how it had all started—how Anderson and his Marxistentializing or rather Trotstentializing colleagues had booted Thompson and the native-culture crowd. For this is what it had really amounted to—a struggle between a European chauvinism masquerading as "Western Marxism", "existentialism" and later "structuralism" and "Althuserianism" versus a "provincial" English form of chauvinism, in the old tradition. Thompson's essay, for all its accuracy in pinpointing just how wrong Anderson was, is written not from a Marxist, but from a basically English chauvinist, standpoint. He rejects Anderson's essay not because it is based on pseudo-Marxism, a falsification of Marxism, but because it is not *English* enough. "For what their scheme lacks (that of Anderson and his collaborator Nairn) is the control of "grand facts", Thompson concludes, "and English is unlikely to capitulate before a Marxism which cannot at least engage in a dialogue in the English idiom."[4] Even the terms chosen by Thompson—'capitulate' and 'English idiom'—are significant. And what this 'English idiom' turns out to be is no more that the already too familiar philosophic-literary-cultural moralizing of the much revered "English tradition"[5].

Thompson's bias is revealed in such statements as: "We can only describe the social process—Marx showed in *The Eighteen Brumaire*—by writing history. And even so, we shall end with only an account of a *particular* process, and a selective account of this."[6] This is empiricism with a vengeance, and in the most vulgar, bourgeois tradition which Anderson is right in characterizing as a crippling sickness. There is an implicit and total rejection of theory in such a statement, and leads to a position which, incapable of any prolonged, logical defense, is really not worth the effort one may spend in refuting it. Thompson's other bias, his English-chauvinist tendency, is revealed in his adherence to the romantic anti-industrialism of the 19th English "tradition" and in his identification with Raymond Williams, the chief expositor of that line. It is more for what he calls 'the ruthlessness in their dismissal of the English experience' that he is so upset by the arguments put forward by Anderson and Nairn than by anything else.

The full dimensions of the split within the New Left was explained again by Thompson several years later in an important essay where he went over those events with a strong sense of bitterness and betrayal:

> We (i.e. at the *New Left Review*) reached a point of personal, financial and organizational exhaustion; and at this moment, the agent of history appeared, in the form of Perry Anderson. We were exhausted: he was intellectually febrile, immensely self-concentrated, decisive. We saw, in a partnership with him and his colleagues, an opportunity to regenerate the review and to recuperate our own squandered intellectual resources. We did not, as is happens, anticipate that first expression of his decisiveness would be to dismiss the review's founder from its board.[7]

Then Thompson adds the following remarks which reveal the vulgar, reactionary "ideological"—"English" versus "European"—basis of the dispute:

> We were, it turned, insufficiently "rigorous": which was true. We were confined within a narrow nationalist culture unaware of the truly internationalist Marxist discourse . . . and had attended insufficiently to a particular dialogue between Parisian Marxists and Parisian existentialists.[8]

> Our intellectual culture has for so long been insular, amateurish, crassly empirical, sell-enclosed and resistant to international discourse that the damage done is probably irreparable. But we still have a chance. We are going "into" Europe, and Tom Nairn and other contributors to the *New Left Review* are attempting to teach us the vocabulary which real intellectuals use over there.[9]

As the reference to Europe here indicates the debate was carried over from the cultural to the political sphere, with Britain's entry into the Common Market, which we will discuss in a later section of this essay. Finally, in the Foreword to his 1978 collection titled *The Poverty of Theory*, which includes both the essays we have been quoting from, Thompson *yet again* goes over

the experience of those years explaining what he calls 'the real sense of isolation and even of alienation' that he had come to feel after being removed
from the NLR which was by the 1970's fully into the "Euro-Marxist" market.
Thompson:

> I find, to my surprise, that over these years I have been carrying a banner inscribed
> with "populist socialism". And, in the company of that unlikely "English national-
> ist", Raymond Williams, I have been developing a "cultural nationalism" marked by
> "romantic excess and indiscriminate empiricism" (I cull this wisdom from Tom Nairn,
> *The Break-up of Britain*, 1977, pp. 303–304).[10]

And the bitterness comes over again, this time to the point of abusiveness:

> But I don't apologise too much. The sense of isolation was real, this was my way of
> getting out of the tent; and I had to write it in that way [referring to the "Open Letter
> to Leszek Kolakowski" essay]. For some years the intellectual "Left" had been in a
> state of overheated paranoia . . . Every Pharisee was being more revolutionary than
> the next; some of them had made such hideous faces that they are likely to be stuck
> like that for life . . . There have been a few signs in the last year or two, that some
> part of the intellectual left has been regaining its reason. It is in this hope that I am
> publishing this book.[11]

Thompson's alienation from the NLR which he recounts in the "Open
Letter" essay was clearly not on socialist grounds. The "Letter", in fact, can
only be described as exemplary correspondence between an English renegade and a Polish renegade. Both started out as Thompson himself admits as
'voices of Communist revisionism of 1956', and each in his own way moved
on to become a renegade. Kolakowski, which it is part of Thompson's "Open
Letter" to explain, moved on to writing banal cold war anti-Marxism in such
CIA organs as *Encounter* and various other reactionary forums. Thompson—
who draws the holier-than-thou posture of his essay from not having degenerated to *that* level—moved on via cultural chauvinism[12] and anti-Marxism
of a "leftist" variety to end up in the ranks of none other than that bulwark
of British imperialism—the Labor Party. It has turned out in the last three
years that, in fact, those 'few signs' by which Thompson measures how far 'the
intellectual Left has been regaining its reason' is no other than their nearness
to joining the ranks of that party.[13] So from a 'communist revisionist' in 1956
to a "New Leftist" in 1960 to a Morrisist or a Williamsite or whatever brand
of cultural-chauvinist in the sixties, and finally to a latter-day Labor Party
entryist. This may not be the classical path of a renegade, but it certainly is
no path to be proud of.

Anderson's reply, "Socialism and Pseudo-Empiricism"—also titled on the cover of No. 35 of NLR, 1966, as "The Myth of Edward Thompson"—which closed the debate, is significant not for any defense that it puts up for his original arguments and methodology, but for what it reveals about Anderson's own "theoretical" prejudices and his own specific conception of British culture. The dialogue—which was not of any real scientific worth in the first place—died out with this essay. Thompson did not reply, and no one else participated. Ostensibly about the course of British history over the period of three hundred years, it really was about the cultural prejudices of Perry Anderson versus those of Edward Thompson. It is not Anderson's historical and philosophic fallacies, nor Thompson's rebuttals followed by his own counter-fallacies, that are of any importance now. What matters generally, as well as for the specific purpose of exploring our theme of cultural criticism, is that they took, or seemed to take, opposite sides in a cultural debate that amounted essentially to no more than a confrontation of English cultural chauvinism with a slightly wider European chauvinism.

Two statements, however, appear in Anderson's essays that further clarify the nature of the "antagonism". The first is an important declaration of faith that warrants a somewhat lengthy citation:

> The theoretical lineage of our work [here Anderson includes his fellow editor Tom Nairn] is altogether different from Thompson's image of it. It comes from the major tradition of Western European Marxism since the First World War—a tradition which has consistently been coeval with new forms of idealism, and a dialectical response to them within the evolution of Marxism itself . . . In the early 1920's Lukacs . . . In the 1930's Gramsci. . . . In the fifties and early sixties Sartre . . . The different histories and trajectories of many other thinkers are also of the greatest importance: Marcuse, Goldmann, Della Volpe, Adorno, Bloch, Althusser.[14]

There we have the program the NLR under the editorship of Perry Anderson over the period of fifteen years or so, all to be "refuted" in the end by none other than Perry Anderson himself in his critique, *Consideration on Western Marxism*. Anderson's second statement concerns Britain and the by now obligatory homage to Raymond William:

> In Britain, however, there has been no coherent tradition of Marxist thought at all . . . In fact, setting aside the question of our own theses, it is virtually certain that any creative Marxist theory in England will follow the pattern I have described (i.e. Marxism mixed with idealism). For the most advanced socialist thought in England is Raymond William's superbly intricate and persuasive work—itself the most generous and humane . . . etc.[15]

The rest should be familiar by now. There is after all one big area that Anderson and Thompson agree on—and that is Raymond Williams. Except that for Thompson, Williams is the foundation, the framework and permanent symbol of the New Left (as incorporated and identified with E.P. Thompson, of course) whereas for Anderson, he is the beginning of the merger of English and European "Marxism" (as performed through Perry Anderson, of course). How this merger takes place we don't find out until Anderson's "masterpiece", his third and most significant essay in this debate, comes out two years later.

The Fallacies of Perry Anderson

Anderson's essay, "Components of the National Culture", published at the height of the student movement in 1968, has created an even bigger "stir" among the British intelligentsia, and is of even more direct relevance to our subject. This time Anderson is more successful—the object of his investigation is more immediate and more tangible than in his "Origins" essay and his methodology is more concrete and anchored to facts. His failure this time is conceptual—it lies in his basic inability to understand the scientific meaning of the term "national culture" which is crucial to his argument. He is condemned by this failure—which stems from his basic anti-Leninist outlook—to oscillate between the poles of a broad European brand of chauvinism and an insular English variety. Before demonstrating this assessment of the essay, we shall begin by looking at its positive aspects.

Written in a period of revolutionary upheaval, the essay makes some accurate observations on the state of bourgeois culture in Britain. These remarks, though by themselves not original in any way, were significant in that, for the first time, they were emanating from within the ranks of the British intelligentsia itself.

In the opening paragraph, Anderson describes his work as a part of "a direct attack on the reactionary and mystifying culture inculcated in universities and colleges, and which it is one of the fundamental purposes of British higher education to install in students".[16] These words contain no new discovery of course, but they still remain strong and salutary words for an English intellectual. "Britain, the most conservative major society in Europe," Anderson continues, "has a culture in its own image: mediocre and inert". The verdict is accurate, though we are beginning again to see the same vulgar comparativism creeping in. We begin to question at this early stage

Anderson's key term "culture"—Does it refer to ruling class culture (which it clearly does in this statement), and then how are other European hegemonic cultures any less 'mediocre and inert' (and wouldn't imperialist and racist been the more appropriate epithets, being expressive of the *content* rather than the mere form of these cultures?) than the British variety? And if he is talking about the "alternative" culture, then in what way is the European variety so superior to the British? The problem arises basically because Anderson does not have a class concept and a class analysis of culture. The opposition on which his essay is built is between British culture and European culture, a national and not a class opposition, and between "British Marxism" (or lack of it, according to Anderson) and "European Marxism", thus turning this most openly class-based of all ideologies into a *national* product, almost an intellectual export commodity by which one can measure whether Britain is being intellectually competitive.

Anderson is on better ground when he distinguishes his own sociological use of the term culture from that 'culture as a whole way of life' definition carried over by the New Left from Eliot and the reactionary literary tradition:

> What is meant by culture here? A preliminary delimitation is essential. We are not concerned with the anthropological conception of culture, as the sum of social customs and symbols in a given society. The generalization of this use of the term characterized the Left in the fifties, and was responsible for some important insights into British society: this was the moment of Richard Hoggart's *Uses of Literacy*. But this usage also blurred the specificity of the superstructural complex which is a society's original thought and art.[17]

In spite of the obligatory reference to the unsubstantiated "important insight" of the earlier Left, this is a step forward. We are finally, it seems, rid of those pseudo-notions of 'community' and 'working class culture' à la Hoggart and Williams, and we are back to culture as a *product* of society not as opposed to society (as in the title of Williams' book), and may be even, we hope, a *class* concept of culture. But our hopes are soon dashed.

Anderson's essay is torn by a basic inner contradiction that stems from this very absence of a class concept of culture. We soon find out that we will not be given any class analysis of the various segments of British national culture, and the ways in which they reflect the course of the struggle between classes in British society, as we would have expected from any scientific essay claiming to clarify, in Anderson's words, 'the specificity of the superstructural complex.' Nor are we offered an analysis of the forces determining the shape of each particular segment of the superstructure, e.g. philosophy, history, literary criticism, etc., because we are told, in a pitiful imitation of the Levi-Straussian structuralist dogma, "the structure of British culture is essentially to be located in the inter-relationship between the disciplines which compose it, and not within each discipline."[18] What we get instead is a vulgar comparativist oscillation between European culture and English culture.

As such a methodology could not be of any scientific value or lead one very far, Anderson states his major thesis, without much preparation, from the start: "Britain, then, may be defined as the European country which—uniquely—never produced either a classical sociology or a national Marxism. British culture was consequently characterized by an absent centre." This is the famous absent center thesis which created such a "stir" among the New Left intellectuals in Britain. It lay behind the crusade that the NLR took it upon itself to propagate what it called "Western Marxism" over a decade and half—all to be later "refuted" by Anderson himself. As for sociology—well, look at all the sociology departments that have mushroomed in the British universities. Now that the center is filled, what next? Is bourgeois British culture any more revolutionary, and any less mediocre and inert? Has the genuinely "national" brand of Marxism, so badly lamented by Anderson's essay, and now after some fifteen years fully provided by none other than Anderson, Thompson, Williams, etc. really conquered "the reactionary and mystifying culture inculcated in the universities and colleges" or has it, the inescapable conclusion, replaced it by another, no less reactionary and mystifying "left" and pseudo-Marxist culture? From F.R. Leavis to Raymond Williams to Perry Anderson, from *Scrutiny* to *New Left Review*—the names and the format are different, but the content is the same.

It is not very fruitful to meet Anderson on any genuinely scientific ground—his method is arbitrary, vulgar comparativist and based on a pseudo-scientific notion of structure. His method, as in the historical "Origins" essays, is not based on empirical observation and on full examination of the total evidence (though not as blatantly) but on arbitrary selection, and comparison, to fit a pre-determined model. Except that here even basic terms do not stand up to scrutiny. What is meant by *classical* sociology? If one defines it as excluding Spencer and any other British sociologist—then obviously it is something Britain never had. The pattern is pre-determined. Similarly with Marxism. If the term is used to cover only Europeans like Lukacs, Gramsci, Altusser, etc. and to exclude people like Christopher Caudwell, V. Gordon Childe, George Thomson, or Maurice Dobb, then obviously one can deny Britain had any "Marxism" and so on.

The best approach is to meet Anderson on his own ground and simply point to the basic fault of his system, the lack of a class perspective, which philosophically manifests itself in his substitution of the idea of totality for the idea of contradiction and of abstract idealist theory for practice. We shall now proceed to examine these more closely.

The reason why Anderson is so sensitive to the absence of sociology in British culture is that he regards sociology as capable of producing what he calls a "totalizing" system. "Classical European sociology was a synthetic social science," he declares, "This is its crucial, innovating importance. Weber's sociology of religion, law and the market, Durkheim's study of suicide and social solidarity, and Pareto's theory of elites, surpassed discrete 'economics', 'psychology', and 'history' by unifying them in a theory of society as a totality".[19] Now for Anderson it does not matter whether this "totality" is idealist or reactionary, so long as it is a totality. Even when it is directly opposed to that other kind of totality, namely Marxism, which Anderson claims to prize so much, it still does not matter. And when this so-called totalizing capacity, found to be so lamentably absent in British culture because it had no sociology, reappears miraculously in imperialist anthropology and in reactionary Leavisite literary criticism—Anderson is overjoyed. British culture is all right, after all. The center was never *really* absent; only misplaced.

The second banal characteristic of Anderson's essay is his handling of Marxism as if it were a national export item, a mere product for competition on the European culture market. Over and over again, we are told that 'Britain . . . produced no important Marxist thinker', that 'it never had a national Marxism', that 'Marxist theory had never become naturalized in England', etc. Marxism is regarded as a set of prescriptions, "sophisticated" philosophic systems and cultural schema to be produced by eminent intellectuals of a particular country to *compete* with those of other countries. It has escaped "Comrade" Anderson that this conception goes against the very essence of Marxism which is *practical and internationalist*, linked as it has been from its inception not to interpretation but to change, not to nations but to classes. He has forgotten the elementary principle that Marxism is not a dogma, but a guide to action, and that Marxism is not produced by this or that would-be world philosopher, but by the practical action of the masses led by the proletariat in their struggle for emancipation. He has forgotten Marx's own words that his theory does not spring from the head of any world reformer, but is based on the observation of the practical struggles of the working class. Anderson's key idea of "national Marxism" is an abominable contradiction in terms. Marxism is not a dogma or a set of doctrines in books. It is *not* national, it is international. There is no such thing as French, German or Italian Marxism; Western or Eastern Marxism. Marxism is one or it is nothing.

So much then for the main contention of Anderson's essay which fails so blatantly in its main conception that had it not touched on our topic of British cultural criticism, and had it not subsequently played such an influential role among the New Left intelligentsia, and, in fact, the British intelligentsia generally, it would have been best to dismiss it as a primitive aberration. But then British cultural criticism as a whole has never been very strong in conceptual framework and by any even elementary standards of rigor, its basic texts whether by Lawrence, Eliot, Leavis *or* by their "Leftist" continuators Williams, Anderson or Thompson, would fall to pieces. It is for this reason that we go into the details of Anderson's faults and inaccuracies, and deal in the rest of this section with the treatment of Leavis in the essay.

As we said earlier, Anderson is overjoyed to "discover" that "British culture" has, after all, produced a "totalizing" discipline in anthropology and in Leavisite literary criticism; he becomes ecstatic his ego having been boosted to new chauvinistic heights. Here at least British culture is triumphant. For British anthropology (no matter that its founder, Malinowski, was a Pole) and Leavisite criticism are the pure, national article. No foreigners and expatriates dominating here. And it is this Britishness that more than compensates for the reactionary nature of both disciplines, and for the fact that they did not differ one bit in ideology and function from the other non-English dominated sectors of bourgeois culture in Britain—e.g., philosophy, history, psychology, etc.

At any rate with Leavis and literary criticism, Anderson finally is on home ground. No more room for the latest continental fashion; the Levi-Straussian-cum-Althusserian "moment" is over; Lukacs and Gramsic must make their exit: the grand English ghost is back:

> Suppressed and denied in every other sector of thought, the second, displaced home of the totality became literary criticism. Here, no expatriate influence became dominant. Leavis commanded his subject, within his own generation. With him, English literary criticism conceived the ambition to become the vaulting centre of 'humane studies and of the university'. English was 'the chief of the humanities.'[20]

On the basis of this "theoretical" framework, Anderson, the "leftist revolutionary" moves on to pay his tributes to Leavis, the rabid reactionary:

Leavis's personal critical achievement, of course, was extraordinary. The rigour and intelligence of his discrimination established entirely new standards . . . There is no need here to demonstrate this: the works speak for themselves. As a critic Leavis is a landmark that has yet to be surpassed.[21]

Words worthy of any common Leavisite. The pseudo-Marxism, the continental name-dropping, the revolutionary phrase-mongering—all that is now openly discarded, and out comes the full-blooded English cultural chauvinism. In the end, this is all that is left for Anderson to stand on—it is the key link that binds the right and the pseudo-left. 'The Great Tradition' marches on. Anderson concludes:

It is no accident that in the fifties, the one serious work of socialist theory in Britain— Raymond Williams's *The Long Evolution*—should have emerged from literary criticism of all disciplines . . . It was from within this tradition (i.e. that of Leavis) that Williams was able to develop a systematic socialist thought . . . The detour Williams had to make through English literary criticism is the appropriate tribute to it.[22]

Britain versus Europe

Tom Nairn's *The Left against Europe?* (1972), although revolving around the specifically political issue of Britain's entry into the European Common Market, is also of immediate relevance to the wider cultural debate which we have been examining in the works of Williams, Thompson and Anderson. Nairn, himself an editor of NLR, seems to have written the book with an eye on that debate. "There is—finally—one other perspective in which the reader may like to situate the essay," he says in his introduction to the Penguin edition, "It may also be seen as a continuation of a polemic within the British left going back to the early 1960's and centred upon *New Left Review*."[23]

As an exposé of the political "left" in Britain, particularly its open degeneration into social-chauvinism on the question of the Common Market, the book makes good reading. Nairn, to his credit, has cultivated the habit of calling a spade a spade more often than most British political "commentators". We are here, however, only concerned with the cultural issues. And here, too, Nairn, is more illuminating, and his judgments less encumbered by the mystifying jargon of his New Left colleagues. This is not to say that Nairn has stepped outside the same Trotskyist, Euro-centric chauvinism of his 'comrades'. His chapters are typically decorated with suitable quotes from the Trotskyist Guru Isaac Deutscher, and substantiated by logic from the continental "thinker"

Ernest Mandel. There is however the fact that, for some reason or other, his remarks on the specifically cultural debate we are concerned with is helpful. Take, for example his accurate characterization of Leavis and Leavisism which is so unlike the adulation heaped upon him by Williams and Anderson. Or, the following remarks on Orwell as the first modern model of ugly English chauvinism (both political and cultural) wrapped in pseudo-left phrases:

> George Orwell's *The Lion and the Unicorn: Socialism and the English Genius* (1940) is the true *locus classicus* of modern British left-wing nationalism in this sense, recording as it does the 'return' of a left-wing intellectual to healthy patriotism and his demand for a socialism based on it . . . Orwell formulated it in unforgettable slogan of British national-socialism: 'No real revolutionary has ever been an internationalist.'[24]

And this takes us to Nairn's main argument, namely, that cultural chauvinism has been the common ground of both the right and the pseudo-left in Britain. Raised as a slogan first by George Orwell, it has been largely handed over to the left since the mid-sixties. This is in substantiation of Nairn's thesis that the political "left" in Britain organized and led a chauvinist and jingoistic campaign against the Common Market, which was supported by such "patriotic" anti-marketers of the extreme right as Enoch Powell. And the common father figure of the cultural chauvinists—both of the right and of the left—was none other than the reactionary recluse of Cambridge—F.R. Leavis (Orwell being too obviously tainted with the Cold War smear to fulfill that role any longer). Nairn is again on the right track here:

> This very comprehensive and solid cultural nationalism may be popular and (in England's historical circumstances) even natural to the left. It is not, however, a 'left-wing' phenomenon in the sense of having any special or logical rapport with socialism. To appreciate this, one need only look at the other end of the spectrum, the national-cultural right. On 2 November 1971, some days after the vote on the Common Market entry, a cry of despair found its way into the correspondence page of *The Times*. It was from no other than Professor F.R. Leavis himself, the father of the Cambridge School, the inspirer of a great deal of the modern nation's cultural *Weltanschaung*. The pretext of the Professor's letter was the fashionable issue of pollution which *The Times* (in common with everyone else) had chosen to be responsibly ashamed about at the time. Why worry about the poisonous effluvia of the modern economy, asked Leavis, when so few are willing to face the real problem? The trouble with civilization is not factory waste, but factories; not the aberrations and faults of the modern economy, but economic growth itself . . . where does the Common Market fit into this darkening perspective? . . . The common market, like the USA, stands for the triumph of the Professor's old enemy, Utilitarianism. It represents the death of 'culture'. . . etc.[25]

So here is where the old Leavisite defense of the 'organic community', pre-industrial and purely English, links up with the "leftist" cultural chauvinism of a Raymond Williams—somewhat refined along the way, as Nairn correctly explains,[26] through the work of the German sociologist, Ferdinand Tonnies. Of course, by 1972, Williams had come a long way from *Culture and Society*, and his rejection of the Common Market, which his 'formal' abstention on the issue, really amounted to, was based as Nairn points out, on openly "socialist" argument. Yet, it was again falsely socialist and abstractly idealist in a typical Williamsite fashion. It refused to face the concrete issue by posing the abstract alternative of a united, socialist Europe which was hardly on the order of the day. Of course, Williams now was—by virtue of the reasoning he used—openly in the company of the "left", but he was significantly *also* in the company of the likes of F.R. Leavis and Enoch Powell.

Culture and Tradition

The Relationship between the New Left and the romantic anti-industrialism of the 19th Century has often been pointed out, and it is best explained by its chief "theoretician", Raymond Williams, who defined the New Left as "a group of writers and political thinkers, essentially based on the tradition of moral critique of industrial capitalism . . . From this position it is able to attack the Fabian ideology which captured the official Labour Party, and also to take in the general attack on dogmatism within the Marxist tradition."[27]

It is certainly ludicrous that an intellectual movement in the middle of the 20th century, and a "progressive leftist" movement at that, should pass over all the advances in socio-political thinking of the previous 100 years to link up with the stale moralism and the by-gone romanticism of the 19th Century. More than that it seems the perfect recipe for inconsistency and failure. To begin with romantic rebelliousness à la Williams Blake is obviously too primitive and inadequate to build anything on. And when it is supplemented by the social criticism of a Dickens or a Carlyle, the "English Tradition", like any other tradition, in fact, comes up against the towering figure of Marx, besides which it inevitably dwindles both in comprehensiveness and in depth. The only thing that can be done is to take the absurdly contradictory detour of bypassing Marx and proclaiming William Morris, the English socialist, more of a Marxist than Marx himself. And when you come to the 20th century, the problems get even bigger. The intellectuals now are either Marxists or Fabians, and if you don't want any of that, you're landed with reactionaries and proto-fascists like Lawrence, Eliot and Leavis to carry on with the "Tradition" which begins by now to look like a true horror house of mummies.

This, unfortunately, is how the New Left started—upon a mythical tradition. Romantics, social critics and fascists make strange bedfellow, especially when they are meant at the same time to give way to "socialist humanism" and to conduct an interminable dialogue with Marxism. But the myth continues, and even when this "radical" traditionalism, this "progressive" cultural chauvinism, is exploded and the old New Left of Raymond Williams and E.P. Thompson is replaced by the new New Left of Perry Anderson and Co.—*the myth still continues.* After all, the Tradition must go on and revolution is not in the best English manner. As Perry Anderson himself puts it:

> The resonance and strength of its appeal (that of the New Left) derived in large part from its renewal of a long tradition in British history, whose genealogy was traced with great power and intensity in *Culture and Society*, probably the most formative socialist work of this period. This tradition which ran from Blake and the Romantics through Ruskin and Morris to Lawrence.[28]

This ideological confusion of the New Left was a reflection of its contradictory political nature. Created in 1956 'by the twin crises of Suez and Hungary', it soon abandoned the tasks of fighting imperialism and confronting Marxism in a serious way. Instead it jumped onto the bandwagon of the Campaign for Nuclear Disarmament, and became a prisoner of the liberal-humanist ethos of that movement. Subsequently, it lost its strength dramatically when that movement petered out in the early sixties. The ambitions of the New Left turned out to be too big for its boots. It had aimed at becoming a major political movement, but in fact 'it never touched any section of the working class'. Its audience never extended beyond a minority of the middle class. Yet, it remained haunted by its political ambitions. So when the CND started, it put itself at the service of that movement hoping to be able to lead it, and paid the price when it declined. "It had lost the virtues of intellectual energy," so runs Anderson's final verdict, "without gaining those of political efficacy. Theoretical and intellectual work were sacrificed for a mobilizing role which perpetually escaped it."[29]

The 'ambiguous identity' of the New Left, Anderson goes on, became 'subjective confusion' and ultimately 'evasion'. This was expressed dramatically in its "almost complete failure to offer any structural analysis of British society". Instead of a systematic sociology, it relied on 'simplistic rhetoric' about 'the common people'. The idiom it used was 'populist and pre-socialist'. Furthermore, politically "it represented a major failure of nerve and intelligence, an inability to name things as they were, which constantly yielded the initiative to the Labour Right in the polemics between it and the New Left in this period."[30] All this shows that the New Left was inadequately equipped, Anderson concludes, to fulfill its ambition 'to furnish a new socialist synthesis'.

Looking Back

The editorial of the very first issue of *New Left Review* (Jan-Feb 1960) is an appropriate place to end this chapter because it reveals many of the original assumptions that lay behind the founding of the New Left, both the movement and the magazine. Suitably enough the article not only begins but also *ends* with a quotation from William Morris—thus evoking the utopian, humanistic and cultural brand of socialism that was going to be the hallmark of the movement.

NLR, we are told, is an offspring of the amalgamation of the two periodicals: *Universities and Left Review* and *The New Reasoner*, and should be 'an organic growth out of the two different traditions'. It is going to maintain a wide scope beyond the bounds of 'narrow politics' and will try to build up 'the humanist strengths of socialism' in cultural and social terms. Above all, the editorial regarded the chief function of the New Left was to remedy what it called 'the poverty of ideas in the Labour Movement' which stemmed from its belief that the 'clarification of ideas' was an 'urgent task for socialism'. It regarded itself as a 'movement of ideas' and its aims as chiefly educational though not in the 'old, stiff teacher-pupil' classroom manner. It hoped to carry on its educational activities through 'Left Clubs, Tribune societies, informal groups and university clubs' in the hope of turning them into more than just discussion groups to become 'centres of socialist work and activity'. The editorial also hastened to add that such groupings were to run 'parallel to, rather than competing with, existing organizations of the Labour Movement'. The rest of the editorial went on to explain how those grass root groupings would become the 'nerve centre' of socialist activity in the community. The range of activities which it outlined included the Campaign for Nuclear Disarmament (CND), activity among the youth and in the trade unions and support for the New Left candidates of the Labour Party at election time.

From this early statement, it was clear that the contradictory nature of the New Left movement stemmed from two basic contradictory impulses, in (A) that it wanted to be an intellectual movement to remedy 'the poverty of ideas' and at the time, a wide-ranging, mass political movement with all the "routine" political day-to-day work that it entailed, and in (B) that it regarded itself as *in* the Labour Party, but not *of* it. As might have been expected, the first contradiction was quickly resolved when the movement failed politically and gave up all too quickly its grandiose political ambition—organizing working-class youth, controlling the trade unions, etc, to confine itself to being a grouping of intellectuals around a review read by a section of the middle class—mainly teachers and students in the universities and other similar institutions. As for the second contradiction, that was never resolved, and the NLR group, not unlike most other "left-wing" groups in Britain, maintained an ambiguous and ambivalent relationship with the Labour Party.

The specifically academic and cultural character of the NLR movement (a more accurate description since it soon became no more than a number of intellectuals grouped around a journal) as distinct from the other, more political "left" grouping in Britain, becomes apparent also in this very first issue in the form of a dialogue between Richard Hoggart and Raymond Williams, about their *books: The Uses of Literacy* and *Culture and Society*. The conversation is informal enough, but there is clearly a tacit assumption that it is a very important, almost historic, event. (It is dated even to the day). Aside from the elitism implicit in the assumption of two academic intellectuals the role of leadership in such a wide political movement as the New Left claimed itself to be, the conversation was also sufficient indication of the basically limited and intellectualist nature of the New Left movement. Moreover, the dialogue itself reveals that the NLR group even as an intellectual movement, 'a movement of ideas' as the editorial liked to call itself, was limited to the socio-moral prognostications of a number of 19th and 20th Century English figures, as discussed in Williams's book, together with a sprinkling of Marxism (usually to "prove" how rigid and inadequate it is). Williams puts it in this way:

> As I saw the cultural tradition then, it was mainly Coleridge, Arnold, Leavis and the Marxists, and the development really was a discovery of other relationships: Cobbett and Morris, for example, who brought parts of my experience that had been separate before. Getting the tradition right was getting myself right, and that meant changing myself and the usual version of the tradition.[31]

This is the crux of the ideological and cultural doctrine of the New Left as it began. It may seem incredible, but as that first issue of the Review clearly indicates, it seems that it was the effort of *one* individual, 'getting the tradition right' and sorting himself out, that was meant to guide a political and cultural movement with wide-ranging "leftist" ambitions.

Clearly, this could not take the movement very far, and it was not very long before the second major figure of the New Left entered the stage in the person of E.P. Thompson, with an article in the third issue of the Review, titled "revolution". It must have been very much like a bid for power. Just as Williams was the cultural guru of the movement, Thompson was going to be its political mentor. The effort, however, was a failure. The article claimed to re-open the argument between reformism and revolution which was a very unfortunate choice for Thompson, this being one of the most advanced and conclusive areas of socialist political theory. As it turns out, the article contains no more than a rehashing of stale revisionism, about socialist forms growing up peacefully within British capitalism, and opposites like reform and revolution, proletariat and labour aristocracy, merging quietly into each other. The major contradiction in British society, according to Thompson, is not between the proletariat and the bourgeoisie, but between the monopolies and the people. This will be resolved not by smashing capitalism, but by fostering what he calls 'societal instincts'.

Paradoxically, Thompson's article created an uproar which even by bourgeois political standards was pedestrian. Yet, the NLR soon capitalized upon it and opened a discussion—continued over the following three issues—which succeeded only too well in keeping to the level of the original article. It contained either servile endorsements like "gone forever are the days of revolution" or gems like "socialism is in contradiction to individual liberty", etc.

Things, however, must have been happening silently in the NLR. By the sixth issue, E.P. Thompson returns with another article, titled "Revolution Again—or shut your ears and run", which reveals the new developments. What these amount to, as one can gather easily from the article, is an attempted takeover of the NLR by the Trotskyists. It is clear that Thompson's position must have been widely challenged, and that he may even have contemplated 'shutting his ears and running'. As he puts it rather bluntly:

> I am getting bored with some members of "Marxist" sects who pop up at Left Club meetings around the country to demand in a your-money-or-your-life tone of voice whether he "believes in" the class struggle, and whether he is willing to give instant adhesion to this or that version of the Creed.[32]

At the end of the article, and after several contemptuous references to the working class and to what Thompson calls 'diabolical and hysterical materialism' he offers his truce, based on three points: To stop using "Marxism", at best to stop using it as a criterion for distinguishing people and, finally, to give up all bias in favor of the working class. This was the sum of the 'new movement of ideas' achieved by the NLR in the first year of its existence.

These discussions, however, completely disappear from the pages of the journal in its second year. The movement of ideas comes to a standstill. Fundamental questions of the movement's outlook are not alluded to except in the long review of Raymond Williams's *The Long Revolution* by E.P. Thompson which we have already discussed. The most significant point about that article is that it is a devastating demolition of the works of Williams. Now if we remember the role that Williams and the "Tradition" he elaborated in his *Culture and Society* are alleged to have played from the first issue of the NLR, in the formation of the New Left movement, we recognize that Thompson's review must have been the signal of an internal crisis. This also explains the Williams cult built in that very article, which has continued on the pages of the NLR ever since. Clearly no movement could admit the fallaciousness and the crippling weakness of its founding ideology (even if that was widely recognized, and openly demonstrated). For the sake of the movement, the cult must go on, and Raymond Williams must not be dislodged.

The character of the NLR by then had changed considerably, as the New Left movement with the sort of ambitions that it outlined in its first editorial had virtually disintegrated. By 1962 it contained hardly anything that was directly political. Instead it became very much like any other academic/cultural review with a slightly leftist slant. It contained, for example, discussions of such "established" novelists as Iris Murdoch, J.D. Salinger, and Williams Golding, and when it cast its cultural net wider it promoted such American liberals as C. Wright Mills and Lewis Mumford, and Levi-Strauss and the French *nouvelle vague*, which were just then coming into fashion. In fact, it became almost an English version of *The Partisan Review*. As editor, the name of E.P. Thompson was dropped in 1962 to be replaced first by an editorial board, and with number 15 of the review, by Perry Anderson.

Things did not brighten up until the issue of 1964 (No 23) with Anderson's essay, "Origins of the Present Crisis" that opened the debate that we have discussed. The editorial to the following issue (No 24), in fact, clearly indicated that the review regarded this as a new departure that would involve a complete re-thinking of its identity and its future function. With that particular issue—produced no doubt under the impact of the 'prospects for the next Labour Government'—it declared that it was going to become a 'forum of left socialist opinion, and that it was going to perform what it called 'the larger-scale historical analysis' through the 'theoretical contribution' of the NLR editors themselves—namely, Perry Anderson and Tom Nairn in the works that we have discussed in the body of this chapter.

A NOTE ON CHRISTOPHER CAUDWELL

Introduction

Christopher Caudwell is still the most advanced and the most revolutionary literary and cultural critic in Britain. In bourgeois and pseudo-left circles there has been a conspiracy of silence regarding his works, and although the enmity has taken a variety of forms and indirect strategies from outright dismissal to misrepresentation to qualified praise for the wrong reasons, the result aimed at has been one and that is to dislodge Caudwell and to prevent his works from exerting their beneficial influence on literary studies.

Caudwell's works that deal with literature and culture are *Illusion and Reality* (1938), *Studies in a Dying Culture* (1938), *Further Studies in a Dying Culture* (1949) and *Romance and Realism* (1970). Together, these works contain the beginnings of a Marxist analysis of the old bourgeois literature in England as well as some of the major modern figures. *Studies in a Dying Culture* was the first fully-developed Marxist critique of such modern bourgeois writers as H.G. Wells, Bernard Shaw and D.H. Lawrence. It set up the correct standpoint from which one should confront modern English writers and the modernist movement in literature generally. With the exception of Mirsky's The *Intelligentsia of Great Britain* (1935), which applies the same kind of critique on a wider scale, there is nothing comparable in English literary criticism. The critique of English bourgeois literature and culture must still begin where Caudwell left off.

A revolutionary literary theory will only come about through struggle against reactionary ideas in the field. This is where Caudwell's contemporary as well historical significance lies. A great deal of pseudo-progressive literary and cultural analysis is still permeated with the direct influence of the reactionary modernist writers. A comparison of *Studies in a Dying Culture* with Raymond Williams' widely known *Culture and Society* published exactly twenty years later reveals how totally opposed the two works are in dealing with very similar subject-matter.

Although it became impossible since the 1951 *Modern Quarterly* discussion to deny Caudwell's unique place in the British literary and cultural field, the tendency since the late fifties has been to misrepresent him and to falsify the general effects of his works as a whole. The roots of this tendency, however, go back, as we shall see later, to the 1951 discussion itself.

A recent study, Dave Laing's *The Marxist Theory of Art* (1978), for example, which devotes a full four pages to Caudwell, emphasizes the "modernity" of his esthetic theory attributing it to the beneficial influence of Freud—a conclusion that greatly delights the writer and seems to assure him that British Marxist theory has not been so bad after all! On the other hand, he completely dismisses the most advanced aspects of Caudwell's literary criticism describing it as a 'hectic account' that is 'mundane in comparison with (the) general theory'. What is odd indeed, and perhaps in its way quite revealing of this and other similar pseudo-left studies, is that Laing implies that the limitation of Caudwell's discussion of bourgeois freedom as expressed in works of literature derives ultimately from the *Communist Manifesto*! Ranking a reactionary pseudo-scientist like Freud so much higher than Marx is only characteristic of the pseudo-left.

Illusion and Reality

The uniqueness of *Illusion and Reality* has been widely, though often grudgingly, admitted. In his brief introductory note to the book, George Thomson has described it as "one of the great books of our time". Published in 1937, it is still the unsurpassed work of literary theory produce by an English writer, and even in the wider context, it still remains a considerable achievement in its field. What is so striking about the work is mainly how accurate Caudwell's judgments are on the literary and artistic trends of his time and secondly, how close he was, through his deep understanding of the essence of Marxism, to the Marxist-Leninist literary and cultural theory. Unlike so many of the latter day so-called "Western Marxists", many of Caudwell's ideas were actually reinforced and not refuted by the subsequent developments of Marxist literary and cultural theory.

This becomes quickly apparent in the brief introductory pages which deftly illuminate the course of Marxist literary criticism in the English context and distinguish it from other literary and philosophic "approaches", like formalism and positivism. Caudwell reveals his superiority to common bourgeois criticism by linking the seemingly autonomous literary viewpoint to a very successful elucidation of the philosophic fallacies of idealism and mechanical materialism. Moreover in doing this, he points to the central concept of Marxist cultural theory, namely, that the fallacies of the old philosophy are basically due to the social division of labor that gives rise to a privileged "class" of philosophers in the first place. Elsewhere in the book he also demonstrates his clear grasp of the effects of the social division of labor in the artistic sphere and of the centrality of this issue for Marxist esthetics.[1]

Caudwell clearly demonstrates that a major part of what it means to be a Marxist in the literary context is to be a fervent opponent of formalism, the most common reflection in this sphere of the twin philosophic fallacies of idealism and mechanical materialism. By pretending to eliminate the subject, both as the producer and the "consumer" of literature, formalism adopted a position toward the literary work that was similar to that of mechanical materialism toward nature. And by elevating the "work of art" to a domain totally independent of concrete reality, governed by laws that were in no way determined by or related to those of human society, it echoed philosophic idealism. Therefore, Caudwell starts out by declaring his opposition to what he calls "a common assumption of literary criticism" and what is certainly the plague of bourgeois literary criticism and specifically of the Anglo-Saxon lit. crit. establishment, namely that "the sources of literatures are irrelevant or unimportant, and that literature can be completely criticized in terms of literature."[2]

The body of Caudwell's work traces the development of poetry from its origins in primitive communist society through the various stages of class society until the present day, which for Caudwell was the thirties. It uses English poetry in its central chapters to illustrate what happens to poetry under capitalism and ends with theoretical chapters on "the characteristics of poetry", the poet's "dream-work" and the position of poetry among the other arts. Finally, in the magnificent last chapter on "the future of poetry", it attempts to explain the position of literature and the writer in the epoch of the socialist revolution. As the work of a young man that is so pioneering and so totally without precedent in the English literary context, the work no doubt has its inadequacies. Yet, on the whole, it remains still in advance of all the more "sophisticated" works produced under the cover of leftism and even of Marxism by people like Laing, Eagleton, Williams and others, and closer to the spirit and essence of Marxism than any of them. In fact, Caudwell should not be bracketed at all with that generation of critics, for while he is basically a Marxist and a Communist, they are not.

Throughout the work, Caudwell comes up with very accurate judgments on important literary and cultural issues, that distinguish him clearly form the common bourgeois and pseudo-leftist English critics—issues like the relationships between culture and the division of labor in society (p. 38), the varieties of the bourgeois "revolutionary" and the bourgeois artist (p. 91–2), capitalist mass culture (p. 107), surrealism (p. 111), Freud (p. 164), science and art (p. 169), the social function of literature (p. 261–2), and culture and communism (p. 293).

Where Caudwell comes into the most direct confrontation with bourgeois esthetics and bourgeois art, however, is in the last chapter entitled "The Future of Poetry". Caudwell examines the contemporary situation which he characterizes socially as one of permanent crisis in which the rise of permanent unemployment will spell its doom. And it is here that his remarks are most in line with the subsequent developments in Marxist literary and cultural theory. Briefly, Caudwell argues that the bourgeois artist in the modern epoch when facing the proletariat has three possible choices; opposition, alliance or assimilation. The first would ultimately lead him to the fascist camp. The second position is very unstable and self-destructive (Caudwell describes it as "anarchist, nihilist and surrealist"), and could not be sustained for long. In the end it must succumb to either one or the other of the two positions. This is especially true of artists if they want to remain artists for, as Caudwell sums it up very accurately, "there is no classless art except communist art, and that is not yet born; and class art today, unless it is proletarian, can only be the art of a dying class."[3]

This takes the artist to the third position that he might take vis-à-vis the proletariat—namely, assimilation. It is precisely here that Caudwell reveals his deep understanding of Marxist cultural theory and practice, when he shifts the focus of attention from the work of art to the artist himself. In fact, the question here begins to concern not only artists but intellectuals in general.

In words that clearly foreshadow subsequent Marxist developments in the theory and practice of the remolding of writers and intellectuals, Caudwell explains how the task of transforming the artist's ideological outlook will be the key to the production of new, genuinely proletarian art. The passage—where he is addressing the artist—deserves a lengthy quotation:

> Our demand—that your art should be proletarian—is *not* a demand that you apply dogmatic categories and Marxist phrases to art. To do so would be bourgeois. We ask that you should *really* live in the new world and not leave your soul behind in the past . . . It is a demand that you, an artist, become a proletarian *leader* in the field of art; that you do not take either of these easy roads which are in essence the same—mechanically shuffling the outworn categories of bourgeois art or mechanically importing the categories of other proletarian spheres. You must take the difficult creative road—that of refashioning the categories and technique of art so that it expresses the new world coming into being and is part of its realisation.[4]

It is a measure of Caudwell's clear understanding of the issues that he declares that here theory must stop and practice take over. The artist, like the scientist or the engineer, can no longer simply rest with arguing his case. "The debate," as Caudwell says, "cannot be solved in theory." It is only through the concrete and daily struggle against bourgeois ideology and bourgeois consciousness, in his own make-up, and which can be achieved not theoretically but through integrating practically with the proletariat and with the socialist revolution, that the intellectual can succeed in participating in the production of new proletarian culture. This, as Caudwell recognizes, is not an easy feat. But arduous as it may be, it is the only road available for the revolutionary intellectual and, furthermore, it is one that for Caudwell had already been demonstrated by the concrete effects of the October Revolution on artists and intellectuals in the Soviet Union.

Studies in a Dying Culture

Studies in a Dying Culture is without doubt a landmark in the history of British cultural theory. At the same time, it is a uniquely isolated work blooming there in the thirties, a Marxist flower midst the desert of bourgeois cultural apologia that covered the field in the succeeding decades. This is the primary point that has to be made and re-emphasized in connection with Caudwell's book—that it is the work of a committed Marxist who, unlike the common British literary critic and cultural commentator, has broken completely with bourgeois ideology and bourgeois thought. The figures Caudwell chooses to discuss—Shaw, Wells, the two Lawrences (D. H. and T. E.), Freud—are not regarded, as is the practice of the bourgeois book on similar subjects, as grand thinkers or great writers who in one way or another are saviours of civilization and of humanity, but as different manifestations of a general sickness of bourgeois civilization and the symptoms of the decay of its culture.

Caudwell never loses sight of the social and political implications of the writings of those figures, while all the time revealing his understanding of the unique way in which the disease surfaces in each of them. The opening essay on Shaw is a good example. Here, in the space of not more than twenty pages, the key traits of Shavism are laid bare clearly and unequivocally. All the main things that need to be said about Shaw are said without mincing any words: Shaw's anarchism, his Fabianism and later his social fascism (e.g. in his openly expressed admiration for Mussolini); his elitist, proto-fascistic utopianism; the failure of his plays as drama and their reduction to an interminable schoolboy debate; his failure also as a real thinker and his subsequent refuge in buffoonery instead, and, finally, his ultimate careerism and opportunism. Caudwell is particularly good in analyzing Shaw's relationship with the bourgeoisie—how he begins by *seeming* to attack it and then, having failed to break with it, returns shamefacedly to its ranks and ends up a mocking and pathetic mirror-image of the same despised bourgeoisie that he now begins to delight. Caudwell also makes a particularly instructive comparison of Shaw with Marx who was ignored or vilified by that same class which delighted in Shaw as a kind of court jester. Because Shaw had read Marx early in his life and knew the alternative that Marxism offered him, he never accepted the necessity of overthrowing the system entirely with all the hardship and sacrifice that it entailed, but was content with posing as the critic of the system while enjoying all the "good things" it rewarded him with. This is the central contradiction of Shavism and the principal manifestation of its expression of the disease of bourgeois culture. Thus, as Caudwell rightly says "Shaw himself, who discovered the ruling class was rotten to the core, and built on the exploitation of the workers, yet ends by marrying ideologically money, respectability, fame, peaceful reformism and ultimately even Mussolini,"[5] and it is his final choice to side with the bourgeoisie in the epoch of its decay and decline that lies behind "the unreality of his plays, their lack of dramatic resolutions, the substitution of debate for dialectic, the belief in life forces and thought Utopias, the bungling treatment of human beings in love, the lack of scientific knowledge, and the queer strain of mountebank in all Shaw says, as of a man who in mocking others is also mocking himself because he despises himself but despises others more."[6]

Similarly, in the essays on D.H. Lawrence and H.G. Wells, Caudwell points successfully to the distinctive ways in which the striving to climb into the world of bourgeois culture was their ultimate undoing. For all their outward rebelliousness, both writers were driven by the same petty bourgeois fear—and in the case of Lawrence, in fact, often intense hatred—of the proletariat, and by the desire to be accepted by the high bourgeoisie. The other essays in the book reveal T.E. Lawrence, as the epitome of the bourgeois man of action in the epoch of imperialism, to be a charlatan and an imperialist agent and himself, in fact, "the plague" and the carrier of "the deadly disease" to an otherwise "healthy land" rather than its romantic saviour as portrayed in imperialist propaganda. Finally, the generally religious, mystical and anti-scientific nature of Freudism is exposed and his advocacy of instinctual "liberation" which he shares with so many other bourgeois "thinkers" of the epoch is shown to lead ultimately to beastliness.

The great achievement of these brief essays—still unmatched in their clarity and sense of purpose by the hundreds of books of bourgeois exegesis—is the way in which Caudwell demonstrates that failure to break with the bourgeoisie and with bourgeois ideology leads, ultimately, each of the writers discussed, because of the nature of the epoch they lived in, to a fascist solution. This is most obvious in the case of D.H. Lawrence. But Caudwell has no reservations about revealing the Fabianism of Shaw and Wells to be also a brand of social-fascism betrayed often by their openly expressed admiration for Mussolini and for the rule of the intellectual elite. T.E. Lawrence's activism and seemingly romantic heroism is also successfully diagnosed as more akin to the charlatan "heroism" of the latter-day men of action like Hitler and Mussolini and diametrically opposed to the kind of heroism represented by Lenin and the Bolsheviks. Lawrence as the willing servant of British imperialism, in spite of the seemingly romantic and "old world" traits of his character, in fact, pre-figured the fascisti and the "adventurers" of the later epoch. Finally, even Freudism, by its inability to study human subjectivity within a sociological framework—the characteristic malady of all bourgeois thoughts in the imperialist epoch, the inability to face social reality—by its recourse to mystical and anti-scientific notions, by its withdrawal from the future and its appeal to a savage past, and so on, actually "points the way to the Nazism" and "by a strange irony", Caudwell concludes, "Freud becomes the apologist of fascist philosophy which rejects him, which burns his books, and seems repugnant to him."[7]

The sequel to these essays, *Further Studies in a Dying Culture*, (1949), covers a wider area. Published twelve years after Caudwell's death, the second book, however, is not as pioneering as the first one. Because it is a more generalized and theoretical account of the various departments of bourgeois thought—religion, esthetics, history, psychology and philosophy—that does not focus on particular figures, it does not play the same role as the earlier volume in the history of British cultural theory. Still, this is not to say that the work does not offer stimulating reading even today. While nearly everything in it is now widely known and has been said, and perhaps better said, elsewhere, it is worth reading if only to see how Caudwell's youthful mind ranged over these diverse areas in a manner so unprecedented among British writers. Some typically sharp Caudwellian observations that might be mentioned, for example, are his remarks on the capacity of religion to be used as a revolutionary weapon (p. 20), the relationship between knowledge and practice (pp. 94–5), the crucial role of the division of labor in the distortion of human consciousness (p. 117), and the scientific nature of Marxism (p. 155).

Caudwell's last book on literary and cultural matters, *Romance and Realism*, which was not published until 1970, is much more than an elaboration upon the chapters that dealt with English poetry in *Illusion and Reality*. In fact, it is a masterly account, albeit in a generalized and theoretical form, of English literature from Shakespeare to the Nineteen-Thirties that is unique in Marxist literary criticism. In the absence of any really Marxist history of English literature, if asked to recommend one book on the subject one would have to point to this one in spite of its brevity. Caudwell is particularly good in analyzing the nature of the Elizabethan, the romantic and the imperialist epochs in English literature, and on individual writers, he has very sharp observations on Dickens, Hardy, Kipling, and Galsworthy. On the whole the work is very stimulating reading and a strong impetus to further research in the field. By its approach and the wealth of its acute remarks and correct summations, it is worth hundreds of tomes and guides on English literature written by the latter-day Leavisites, Williamsites, and pseudo-Marxists of the lit.crit. industry.

Conclusion

This brings us to the final section of this essay, namely, the way Caudwell has been treated or maltreated by the British literary and cultural establishment. As we said in the opening paragraph, there has been a conspiracy of silence among the bourgeois critics and a campaign of deliberate distortion among the pseudo-leftist ones regarding Caudwell's works, and it is the latter tendency with which we will now be concerned.

The roots of the distortion campaign go back to the *Modern Quarterly* discussion of Caudwell's works. Published in the 1951 issues of the theoretical journal of the then revisionist-turning CPGB, the co-called discussion consisted basically of a denigrating and malicious attack on Caudwell in the opening article, titled "Caudwell and Marxism", by the notoriously revisionist Party "philosopher", Maurice Cornforth. The so-called discussion was not initially meant to be a discussion at all, but a final settling of accounts with Caudwell's revolutionary Marxism as a prelude to an all-out revisionist policy in cultural matters. In spite of George Thompson's spirited defense, "In Defence of Poetry", published in the following issue, which he was suddenly asked to write at very short notice, and in spite of other shorter contributions, the "debate" merely served to expose the Party's revisionism without lessening one bit from Caudwell's real status.

The campaign, however, did succeed in misrepresenting Caudwell and in falsifying the nature of his work, thus setting the tone for the future distortions of the sixties and seventies to which we shall now turn. In fact, the beginning of Caudwell's misrepresentation goes back even earlier, but again from the same source, to that important early Alick West article, "On Illusion and Reality", in the *Communist Review* of January 1948, which ostensibly very pro-Caudwell, actually misrepresented him on the crucial issue of the break with bourgeois culture. While generally highly approving of *Illusion and Reality*—calling it "an important work not only for the study of poetry, but also for the immediate political struggle"—West cannot face the revolutionary conclusions of Caudwell's work and misreads his remarks completely. West's position is particularly ludicrous when he tries to dilute Caudwell's revolutionary rejection of bourgeois culture and to transform it into a bourgeois and later revisionist (à la Lifshitz and Lukacs) spirit-of-the-age concept that opens a back door to welcome the old culture in again.

Thus, the *Modern Quarterly* discussion of 1951 and the ensuing Cold War climate, with which it oddly converged as far as Caudwell was concerned, prepared the ground and set the pattern for his future maltreatment. The irony is that the initial vilification should have come from precisely the quarter that should have cherished him as its own hero. After a total silence that was only occasionally interrupted by a casual dismissal from the literary critical establishment in the heyday of reactionary Leavisism and so-called

"New Criticism", Caudwell was not seriously considered again until the rise of the so-called "New Left" in the late fifties and early sixties. From then on Caudwell's works, while no longer ignored like before, were subjected to an equally damaging treatment that consisted this time of distortion and misrepresentation. Between the Scylla of the Right and the Charybdis of the pseudo-left, Caudwell's works have been almost totally prevented from affecting the course of literary and cultural studies in his own country.

In *Culture and Society 1780–1950*, presumably one of the key texts of the new "leftist" renaissance in British literary and cultural studies, Raymond Williams, with the Cold War and Leavis era not far behind, makes no pretense to hide his deep hatred for Caudwell and all that he stands for. With words that were later to be echoed by other pseudo-Marxist critics like Terry Eagleton, Williams, posing as the champion of Leavisite "concreteness" but actually revealing his deep vulgar-empiricist prejudices, pronounced dismissively that Caudwell "has little to say, of actual literature, that is even interesting" and that "for the most part is not even specific enough to be wrong".[8] It turns out that what really infuriates the pseudo-left and social-chauvinist Williams, as well as his pseudo-Marxist disciples, is actually Caudwell's description of English literature as bourgeois and of imperialist culture as decadent and dying.

In the seventies, the new rising star of the pseudo-left and the author of that abject homage to F.R. Leavis, *The Moment of 'Scrutiny'*, also tried his hand at Caudwell. In an article published in the *New Left Review*[9], Francis Mulhern tries to dress up Caudwell as a forerunner of the degenerate trends of so-called "Western Marxism" of the seventies, a sort of bizarre combination of Althusser and Goldmann. Revealing very early on where he really stands, Mulhern accuses Caudwell of "historicism" which in the current degenerate parlance of "Western Marxism" means adherence to historical materialism. His main aim, however, is to distort Caudwell's works and to "re-arrange" them for the purposes of the pseudo-left. This comes out very clearly in his last paragraph when he says that "Caudwell's insights may be unusable in their original context, but it is far from impossible to devise other contexts in which he could become productive. The point is not *whether* Caudwell is to be read, but *how* he is to be read",[10] (Mulhern's emphasis). So the aim is to emasculate Caudwell, throw away the genuine revolutionary Marxism (that original context Mulhern has in mind) and turn him into yet another pseudo-leftist and "western Marxist" (the other contexts all too readily available for Mulhern). But what for, the question immediately arises, when the market is already over-full with the works of Althussers, Marcuses, Lukaces, etc.? And the answer can only lie in the all too apparent chauvinist impulses of the pseudo-left to look back, at the end of the day, to some "genuine" home product. It is the same old Buy British campaign, in a cultural context, and part of the same search for some British figure to stand his ground against the "Continentals" that contributed so much to the Raymond Williams cult in pseudo-left circles in Britain.

For someone who did not have much love for Continental Marxism in the first place, however, Caudwell would not be of much use in this respect. That is why three years later, E.P. Thompson, that other major Guru of the British pseudo-left, tried to re-fashion Caudwell in a totally different image— his own. This time the attempt[11] was to make him into a revisionist and a renegade like himself which only shows how far the pseudo-left would go to "prove" a prejudice. "Caudwell was potentially a heretic within the orthodox Marxist tradition," Thompson pronounces adding the significant qualification, "He may or may not have known this."[12] *Voila!* To each his own Caudwell. Although Thompson is quite right in saying that Caudwell was no forerunner of "Western Marxism" and "Althusserian idealism" as implied by Mulhern, his own particular kind of distortion is the most damaging of all. Thompson's standpoint is that of an anti-communist renegade who could not, in this context, but be essentially anti-Caudwell also. And this Thompson makes no pretense to hide as when he declares categorically that *Illusion and Reality* is 'a bad book' and that "very much of Caudwell's works, perhaps ninety percent must be set aside. It no longer affords any point of entry."[13]

So from Cornforth—of the 1951 *Modern Quarterly* attack—to Raymond Williams, Francis Mulhern, and E.P. Thompson, that forerunner and standardbearer of any future socialist cultural transformation in Britain has been continuously distorted and vilified by figures supposedly on the left. The only conclusion to be drawn from this sorry state is that the hatred of Caudwell and the enmity toward his works can only be regarded as yet another matrix for the bankruptcy of the British pseudo-left and for its complete betrayal of socialism.

· 5 ·

JOHN McGRATH AND THE ALTERNATIVE THEATRE MOVEMENT

John McGrath

John McGrath is one of the leading figures of the "alternative theater" movement in Britain, who has also become one of its main theoreticians. Under the title of *A Good Night out—Popular Theatre: Audience, Class and Form*,[1] he has collected the six talks that he gave at Cambridge University in a book published with a Foreword by Raymond Williams. By British cultural standards these are very sound leftist credentials. Williams, in fact, very efficiently utilizes those few pages to indicate what might be termed the left-boy-network type of relationship between McGrath and himself—how they found their way to the same meeting in Trinity, or how they lost their way in the same corridors in King's, etc. He then goes on to refer in highly laudatory terms to the 'important radical point of view' of those lectures and to McGrath's achievement in 'having learned to some purpose' and in having 'shown the possibility of other plays and other ways'. What this radical point of view is and what this purpose and these other ways are, one is not supposed to ask. The vagueness is deliberate. Either you are "in", and then you would understand and assent, or if you don't understand well then you're simply "out of it". After all isn't it sufficient that the man has had such 'varied experience in prestigious theatres and in television and cinema?' The tone of the Foreword accurately sets up the framework within which we are supposed to read these essays—here we have a man who "has done very well" in the established bourgeois theatre, has worked even on state TV and in Hollywood films, and who at the same time is most suited to tell us about the alternative, the revolutionary, the socialist form of theatre. Truly a man for all seasons. His success with the cultural "establishment" paradoxically does not diminish, but in fact enhances his fitness for the role of the theoretician of the "alternative movement." Confronted with the "dilemma" of the class nature of society and of culture and with the need of the bourgeoisie to universalize its statements—i.e. to present its own particular interests as the *general* interests of humanity—McGrath openly admits that, as a playwright, he inevitably sides with the bourgeoisie: "Well, I'll tell you what most of us do" he says, "—we take the point of view of a normal person—usually that of a well-fed white, middle class, sensitive but sophisticated literary critic: and we *universalize* it as *the* response."[2]

Now as the *values* of the contemporary bourgeoisie, unlike those of the bourgeoisie in its by-gone revolutionary phrase, are so blatantly decadent, reactionary, racist and potentially fascist, they cannot, unlike the older revolutionary values, be openly and explicitly universalized. They have to be mystified to be universally *enforced*. It is this which lies behind the cult of ambiguity and mysteriousness, the pseudo-artistic posture of "not giving any answers" that has been a key characteristic of modernism from its inception all the way to the "meaninglessness" of the Theatre of the Absurd and including, in fact, the kind of deliberate vagueness in the terms Williams uses in his Foreword to McGrath's book. Various types of ambiguity, multi-layered levels of meaning, mythical parables and archetypes, "art must never be paraphrased", "we don't want to tell people what to think", etc. to the end of the familiar jargon of modernist literature and criticism.

What McGrath wants to do is not to confront this decadent, racist culture; not to destroy it and in the process build a new, proletarian culture, but to *co-exist* with it and develop simultaneously, under conditions of imperialism, a working class culture which in his own admission is severely deformed and contaminated by those conditions. This scheme is not only utopian, because it is impossible; it is also essentially reactionary because it leaves the status quo intact. McGrath falls into the same vulgar sociologism of the cultural writings of people like Raymond Williams and Richard Hoggart which substituted the actually existing deformed and contaminated working class culture under imperialism for the proletarian socialist culture that can only be created in the process of the socialist revolution.

Britain is an imperialist country with a labor aristocracy that is strongly entrenched both as a class and ideologically. This labor aristocracy is very skillful at using its dominant position and in manipulating the ideologies of imperialism, social-imperialism, jingoism, racism and even social-fascism in order to maintain its hold over the working class in the service of its bourgeois masters. There can be no proletarian socialist culture peacefully co-existing and peacefully developing and evolving side by side with ruling imperialist culture. Historically all such efforts have failed, and the lesson of that history is written over the years extending for a whole century, from the 1880's to the 1980's. To revive such an approach in the present day can only mean either extreme obtuseness or conscious collaboration.

Now since the theatre is even more obviously social in character than other forms of cultural activity, the mechanics of its incorporation into ruling class culture and of its domination by ruling class ideology can be easily seen. The example of the so-called angry generation of English playwrights—from the mid-fifties to the mid-sixties—is well known. Heralded first as the modern voice of the working class in English theatre, the movement signaled, in fact, nothing more than the rise (or the degeneration) of a number of writers, directors and actors from the working class into the ranks of the decadent, British and Hollywood, bourgeoisie. What it achieved was not proletarian socialist, or even working class, drama, but a new, bourgeois drama that contained, and only in part, some aspects of working class life in a decaying, imperialist society. Therefore, as a "revitalized" form of bourgeois drama, there was nothing easier than for it to become an established, respectable and even dominant form of drama, which it did in an exceptionally short period of time.

McGrath, by his admission, followed this very course, which he describes as 'the Regular Route', and what he learned from it, again in his own words, was "no more than the elaboration of a theatrical technique for turning authentic working-class experience into satisfying thrills for the bourgeoisie."[3] Sociologically, McGrath concludes, he was one among a whole generation of 'bright young working-class youth, thrown up by the 1944 Education Act' into the arms of the ruling class to be exploited for its service. And, McGrath implies, with good rewards.

McGrath now is disillusioned with this kind of drama, and claims to reject it completely. As a "theoretical" justification, he even produces against what he calls the 'idealist' literary conception of drama as text his own 'materialist' way of looking at drama as:

An evanescent, unrecordable act of communication between two groups of people present in person in the same space on the same night; and that the communication took place in many areas including the price of tickets and the content of the programme.[4]

Now if McGrath wants us to take this as the dialectical-materialist conception of drama, which he implies, then it is clearly nothing of the kind, and if it is materialist at all, then it is vulgar materialist or "situationist" materialist, and is meant to endorse McGrath's vulgar-empiricist deformation of proletarian culture into already existing forms of working class culture under imperialism, which he shares with people like Williams. It is merely a pretext for him to claim that proletarian drama is the form of entertainment enjoyed by the working class as opposed to the bourgeois drama of the West End, which workers do not attend. This distinction is made regardless of the content of these presentations which in McGrath's definition is tucked away somewhere with the price of the tickets. In fact, McGrath carries his esthetic "innovation" a step further by implying that it is not content which determines (in the sense of defining the limits of) form, but the other way around. "Elements of the form" he tells us, "are taken quite clearly as signifiers of class content." So as opposed to the bourgeois form of West End drama, we have working class forms (and, by implication, contents) of entertainment ranging from working-men's club entertainment (i.e., bingo, booze, and strip-tease as McGrath describes it), to the Christmas panto and the pop or rock concert, supplemented of course by the film and television entertainment of the kind produced by such Hollywood hacks as Harry Saltzman and Fred Zimmermann who McGrath, as confessed disciple, declares "know more about pace and movement than almost any author since Homer."[5]

McGrath then goes on several pages enumerating what he calls the main features of working class entertainment under such headings as directness, comedy, music, variety, effect, etc., all of which tell us nothing about the class content which it is supposed, according to McGrath, to signify, or the revolutionary socialist aspects which we presume he would be looking for. All that we gather from this detailed list is, in fact, that the workers like a funny, musical and varied sort of entertainment with lots of emotion and local colors, and don't like "two or three long acts of concentrated spoken drama, usually with no more than five or six main characters."[6] The immediate question is, of course, that if it were the other way around, would that have made the second form of drama any less bourgeois and the first any more so. And who can prove that the bourgeoisie are any less fond of racy, musical, varied and emotional sorts of entertainment.

After all this is the very stuff of the established bourgeois genre of musical comedy. The issue then must be determined by the content which remains the decisive factor for establishing the political character of any kind of drama, and, significantly, McGrath has nothing to say about that except in a single sentence that speaks louder than many pages when he states openly "the nature of much working-class comedy is sexist, racist, even anti-working class."[7]

McGrath's position is so clearly contradictory that it cannot be sustained for very long. He is soon forced to admit that:

> There is a danger in schematically drawing up a list of some features of working-class entertainment I am indulging in what is called 'tailism', i.e. trailing along behind the tastes of the working-class, debased as they are by capitalism; and merely translating an otherwise bourgeois message into this inferior language.

And he goes on *undoing* his own list:

> To enumerate once more: directness can lead to simplification; comedy can be racist, sexist, even anti-working class; music can become mindlessness; emotion can become manipulation and can obscure judgments; variety can lead to disintegration of meaning and pettiness; effect for effect's sake can lead to trivialization; immediacy and localism can close the mind to the rest of the world, lead to chauvinism, etc.[8]

Which takes us to the very point that we started from. McGrath's confusion, however, is only *apparently* dispelled. His basic mistake, which consists of observing only the connection but failing to see at the same time *the clear distinction* between existing working class culture and proletarian socialist culture, remains uncorrected. It lies, for example, behind his surprising insistence that, as he puts it: "There *is*, even now in England, an identifiably 'working class' culture which is simply *different* from that bourgeois culture emanating, etc."[9]

Now such a statement is at best a tautology, since working class culture once it is described as the kind of cultural activity that the workers indulge in or, in this case, the kind of entertainment they patronize, has obviously existed ever since the working class came into being, and will remain so long as it remains. How this culture helps or, in some cases *hinders*, the formation of a proletarian socialist culture, as a new and distinct kind of working class culture formed by different social processes and different social conditions is another, and very significant, matter. While it is true that the seeds of the new culture are inevitably located in the present, particularly in the cultural forms that could be renovated and infused with a new content, it is quite possible under imperialist conditions for the proletarian socialist culture even in its embryonic and rudimentary stage to be totally suppressed or go underground for a long time, as under fascism. McGrath's metaphor of 'first sounds' (for existing working class theatre) and 'new language' (for the 'theatre that can never be fully articulate until socialism is created') is again false because it observes only the continuous, developmental aspect of the relationship and not its revolutionary, *rupturing* and discontinuous side. McGrath's refuge in Brecht and Gramsci in support of his argument, in fact, disproves his own case, for the concept of popular culture, approximation even though it was to proletarian socialist culture, was in McGrath's own words *'defined largely by its absence'* under conditions of Nazi Germany and fascist Italy. Fascism, as a period of extreme reaction, can affect a break, however temporary, between existing working class culture and future proletarian socialist culture, almost in a black parody of the way socialist revolution and cultural transformation achieve a permanent, radical break with the debased culture of capitalist society.

It is this crucial error that lies at the root of all the further mystification that plagues the rest of McGrath's book. In the fifth chapter, titled "Theatre as Political Forum" which deals with the content of drama—a hitherto unapproached topic—the faults of the argument become fully apparent as the fog of mystification increasingly thickens. Thus we are told, for example, that the relationship between politics and art changes without tackling the more basic question of what these relations are or should be under socialist conditions and for the socialist playwright. To say that the relationship changes becomes simply a way of evading the issue, and to say that 'every writer who is a writer will be in a constant process of redefining that relationship' is actually running away from the open admission that the relationship between art and politics for the socialist writer could only be one of subordination, i.e. that he must consciously put his art in the service of his politics.

Further on we are told that 'perhaps the most important feature of theatre as a form is that its dimensions are those of the human figure,'[10] which is a different form of the earlier vulgar-empiricist notion of theatre as communication between a group of people in the same place, at the same time. Marxist esthetic theory[11], as McGrath should know, in fact, considers that the theatre and art generally can and should be "larger than life", and "on a higher plane", i.e., that by reflecting human life in a more concentrated way, by typifying contradictions and creating more ideal and, therefore, more universal conditions, art will in turn have a more powerful impact upon reality than by being enslaved to what McGrath calls 'the dimensions of the human figure' (which in the end is always reducible to a naturalistic esthetic).

A little later we are told, this time somewhat pompously, of the need 'to redefine our inheritance for the history of Western civilization', which again merely states the problem and rushes quickly away from it. The issue to begin with is inaccurately formulated—for, in this day and age, to confine civilization merely to 'Western civilization' is nothing but arrant chauvinism. Secondly, 'to redefine our inheritance', actually means nothing unless one does it, and that entails more than just being aware of the rather blatant reactionary machinations of an Ian Trethowan, a Bernard Levin or a Martin Esslin (names actually "dropped" by McGrath himself) and should lead to the conceptualization of a radical break with all forms of exploitative class culture everywhere, together with the simultaneous endeavor to build a new, socialist proletarian culture, a task that too clearly is beyond the horizons of McGrath's imagination.[12]

One of the basic principles of Marxist esthetics is that the content of art, and particularly socialist art, is the decisive factor in an antithetical contrast to McGrath's position that the subject matter can be anything and that the actual choice is not significant, or his earlier "innovation" already mentioned that form is a signifier of class content. The choice of subject matter *is* significant because it is a key indicator of a writer's outlook and of his understanding of the course of struggle in his society. McGrath's totally inadequate treatment and his constant evasion of the issue complement his basic confusion on the distinction between proletarian socialist culture and existing working class tastes and prejudices. Ultimately this stems from his inability to make a scientific analysis of contemporary British capitalism, apparent at a very elementary level in the complete absence in his talks of such key concepts as imperialism and the labor aristocracy that are essential for such an analysis.[13]

What is more aggravating is that the facts of McGrath's biography indicate that he should have at least recognized the primary necessity for analyzing, exposing, fighting and overthrowing British imperialism. After all he started out his adult life by becoming an officer in the British forces first in Germany ("It was an army of occupation. Our job was to show those bastards how to behave"[14]) and later in Egypt during the high anti-imperialist upsurge just before the nationalization of the Suez Canal. There, McGrath was posted in the Canal Zone where, in his own words, they "were being shot at and sniped at . . . and nasty armed guards would be turning over Egyptian villages all through the night, which [he] fortunately, never had to do."[15] Well, even if he hadn't, at least he had seen enough of the way imperialism works at first hand, to warrant describing his almost total silence about it later, however much that silence was shared by the vast majority of the so-called New Left British intellectuals, as nothing but complicity. It turns out, in fact, that McGrath even if he did not rel-ish his army life he was still happy for the chance it gave him to "tour" so many countries and be 'quite grateful for that load of experience'. McGrath's imperial-ist experience was then nothing that he felt guilty about, ashamed of or even wanted to forget about. On the contrary, like Oxford, to which he later went, and like TV and the West End after that, it was all something that he went through, an 'experience' he was 'grateful for' and, it seems, quite well enjoyed.

Out of that army experience came one of his early plays about no less imperialist a theme than a British officer luring a soldier 'into shooting down an Egyptian just for kicks'. This, it seems was the right apprenticeship for the future maker of police-glorifying TV series and Hollywood spy thrillers, which were the next stages in McGrath's career. The rest of the interview which reveals, in addition to McGrath's undue fondness for four-letter words, how, as in the army, he enjoyed each one of those stages, where he was always learning 'how it is done and why it is done', until he finally ends up as a self-proclaimed revolutionary socialist at the head of a self-proclaimed Marxist theatre group, with still 'a lot more to learn, and a long way to go'.

The Alternative Theatre Movement

Aside from the collection of sophomoric essays[16] of a John Arden or the à la Brecht contemplations of an Edward Bond[17], McGrath's talks are virtually the only extended published material on the theory behind the "alternative" theatre movement in Britain. We, therefore, have to turn to the history of that movement particularly in Catherine Itzin's work both in her book, Stages in the Revolution (Methuen—1980), and on the pages of the magazine Theatre Quarterly of which she is one of the two editors.

Historically and politically the "alternative" theater movement in Britain can be linked directly to the New Left Movement, particularly in its second phase following the wide "disillusionment" with Harold Wilson's Labor gov-ernment. The movement can be conventionally divided into two generations. The first generation (writers like Arden, Wesker, Bond, Mercer, Griffiths) was already a spent force by the late sixties, and corresponds politically to the earlier CND generation, to magazines like The New Reasoner and the early phase of The New Left Review, to the work of such New Left "theoreticians" as Raymond Williams, Richard Hoggart and E.P. Thompson; in other words, to that widely discussed group of Labor left and Communist renegade intellectuals whose outlook was decisively altered by the events of 1956. The second generation might be likened to the Trotskyist editorial board of the New Left Review, particularly Perry Anderson and Tom Nairn, who took over after the openly admitted exhaustion of the earlier editors, in a period of despair and disillusionment following the collapse of the CND and later the "betrayal" of the Wilson government. This group soon exhibited all the Trotskyist characteristics, ranging from empty and fruitless theorizing, to shallow cosmopolitanism or rather Europeanism and vulgar academism and most importantly, revolutionary, Marxist phase-mongering covering a deeply reactionary outlook. As an ideology, Trotskyism was even more exhausted and reactionary than the revisionism and Labor Party leftism of the first generation. Historically, of course, it was the older and more vicious trend, but by the sixties it was clearly a spent force with no inner vitality, and it owes its revival largely to the external events of the last years of that decade, particularly Vietnam and the student movement, that put the wind back in the sails of these moribund trends, as well as giving rise to what later came to be called the alternative theatre movement.

One example of the atrophied first generation of "alternative" or "revolutionary socialist" playwrights is Arnold Wesker who was connected with the early cultural campaigns of the Labor Party, complementing the CND and the rise of the New Left. The dismal and disillusioning failure of those campaigns led Wesker to an open acceptance of 'isolation' and 'impotence' in the late sixties and seventies, and to his declaration that he was and probably always has been nothing but an 'old-fashioned humanist', the implication being that it was wrong for him ever to have been described as a socialist. Writers like John McGrath later took on Wesker as a convenient straw man which in the process of putting down they could exhibit their own red credentials. The lesson to be learnt here is that as the Centre 42, the cultural campaign Wesker was connected with, "was a very real forerunner—in theory and practice—of the alternative theatre movement,"[18] the phenomenon of a liberal, even a reactionary, masquerading as a socialist, or exhibiting what McGrath called 'tremulous flirtation with "progressive" ideas', was not something confined to Wesker, but became more of a general characteristic of the alternative playwrights. As we have seen, the grounds for calling McGrath a socialist writer or a socialist theoretician of the theatre are just weak. The only difference is that in McGrath's case the flirtatious relationship with socialism is, so far, still going on.

Unlike McGrath, however, many of the second generation alternative playwrights have followed Wesker's path and, either explicitly or implicitly, broken with socialism. Some have even degenerated into openly attacking it.

But before we go into that, mention must be made of two other illustrative writers. The first is Trevor Griffiths, who as a member of the older generation and a self-confessed disciple of Raymond Williams and E.P. Thompson is perhaps the best example of the worst sort of reactionary reformism in the movement. Under such half-baked slogans as 'strategic penetration' and 'ideological intervention', and taking his "theoretical guidelines" from the works of Raymond Williams, Griffiths tries to justify writing for the most bourgeois theatres, actors and TV serials. It is revealing that such open class collaboration has been described by John McGrath himself as 'principled Marxist interventionism', although it must be added that the defense he puts up for Griffiths' tactics is more in the nature of protesting too much. The absurdity of Griffiths' 'penetrating strategy' becomes fully apparent when seen in the light of the elements that constitute his so-called socialist outlook, in statement like: "My plays are never about the battle between socialism and capitalism. I take that as being decisively won by socialism,"[19] or such profound observations as the one about E.P. Thompson replacing Lenin just as 'socialist humanism' has replaced the 'insurrectionary moment', or the one about the Left taking responsibility for Stalin just as the National Front must take responsibility for Hitler, and other such inanities.

Finally, the case of Edward Bond, another first generation writer, is particularly illustrative because, in a manner strikingly similar to the cult of Raymond Williams in the literary-cultural milieu, so much is made of him which he has so little show for. What for anyone else would have been regarded as backwardness or, at least, an acute ease of late development, for Bond becomes the miraculous decade's growth from 'intuition to consciousness', from 'moralism (whatever that means) to Marxism' and from 'social commitment (whatever that means) to socialist commitment', etc. It seems that it is destined for Bond to be Britain's number one contribution to European drama, just as Raymond Williams has fulfilled that role in Marxism or, for that matter, Kevin Keegan in football. The most elementary of observations become the profound insights of the creative mind when uttered by Bond. Statements like: "We live in a closed society when you need money to live . . . We have no natural rights, only rights granted and protected by money,"[20] "Most established social orders are not means of defending justice, but of defending injustice," and "Our economy depends on exploitation and aggression,"[21] and "Technology is a very valuable thing which is greatly misused."[22] Such statements are quoted so often that they seem to have made Bond convinced enough of his Shavian/Brechtian eminence to write unreadable explications to his plays in the form of Prefaces.

The efforts to build up Bond as The Great English Playwright, just like the so-called policy of 'strategic penetration' or the earlier centre 42 cultural campaign are not just aberrant tendencies in the alternative theatre movement, but point to the basic characteristic of that movement which can be simply described as wanting to have it both ways, to be a threatre for the working class and a theatre for the bourgeoisie at the time, to be, in fact, reactionary and socialist at the same time. The material basis for this seemingly paradoxical and schizophrenic nature is summed up—often by the playwrights themselves—in one word: subsidy. Here we have a self-proclaimed revolutionary socialist movement speaking in the reddest of terms, maintained and supported financially by the very capitalist state it has sworn to overthrow. As Catherine Itzin puts it:

> Alternative theatre—particularly political theater—could not have developed on the scale it did in the seventies without subsidy. This was, from the beginning, one of the fundamental ironies—that theatre companies whose stated aim and *raison d'être* was to do away with the capitalist state and its institutions (including the Arts Council of Great Britain) and replace it with a socialist society could only work to achieve those ends with financial assistance from the hated state.[23]

This, however, was no mere irony or 'minor tension' as Itzin calls it. There were definite political strings attached: Apparent, for example, in the clear stipulation that no theatre group that was connected to a political party was eligible for receiving money. Therefore, it was not a mere innocent paradox, as one of the groups describes it, or "a contradiction that had to be lived with", as another sums it up as if justifying the inevitable. Subsidy money was more than a paradox and a contradiction; it was the established, almost the inevitable, way of life for this so-called revolutionary theatre. What sustained it materially was not the people, but the state which could at any time also bring it to a halt. Itzin concludes, reflecting on the changing economic climate, "as subsidy had been crucial to the growth of political theatre, so it would be instrumental in its decline."[24] Linked as it was financially, and, by implication, politically, to the imperialist state, the so-called alternative theatre could only be regarded as the opposite of what it proclaimed. In the words of Itzin again: "Assessed on its own terms—on its own desire to achieve a socialist society—the political theatre movement could only have been judged a failure."[25]

In the final pages of this chapter, we want to demonstrate that even politically the movement was as near to socialism as the Arts Council is to a revolutionary institution or the Governments of Wilson and Callaghan were to a socialist government.

First of all, nearly all of the playwrights and groups in the alternative theatre movement are plagued by that most vulgar form of anti-communism, namely anti-Stalinism—that favorite theme of the bourgeois media since the days of George Orwell which has been reappearing more and more frequently in the era of the so-called New Cold War. Thus we see a David Mercer railing so uncontrollably against Stalinism and its 'ugly consequences—the corruption and degradation of both art and artists' that he insists on doing away with all Marxist, and 'indeed any kind of philosophical or ethical model' altogether.[26] Consequently, this self-proclaimed Marxist slips all too easily into the decadent aestheticism of the 'writing itself as a process of inquiry' kind of posture. Or, we have the aforementioned Trevor Griffiths proclaiming that socialism is already achieved, and all that remains to be done is 'to take responsibility' for the evil deeds of Stalin, just as those in the National Front (can they be around with socialism already achieved?) must take responsibility for Hitler; or a Howard Brenton who regards his primary task as 'informing' people about Stalin though admittedly, he adds, "there is the risk of what you say being abused by the right-wing press."[27] In fact, it soon becomes clear that the political *bête-noire* of the alternative theatre writer is not imperialism or capitalism or the pseudo-socialism of the Labor party or even Hitler and the European neo-fascism but a great (despite his mistakes) leader of the proletariat. Furthermore, the nature of this vicious attack on Stalin is clearly anti-Communist because it is not a critique of Stalin as contrasted say, with the Marxism of a Lenin or a Mao; it is, in fact, a blanket condemnation that contains the rejection of communism, of Leninism and of the very basics of Marxism. It comes as no surprise then that so many alternative writers and groups have had links with Trotskyist sects, like the connection between CAST (Cartoon Archetypal Slogan Theatre) and the playwright David Edgar with the Trotskyist IS (International Socialism), or have developed under the general influence of Trotsky, like the playwrights David Mercer, Trevor Griffiths and Howard Brenton. It should also not be surprising to have the all-too-frequent case of the alternative playwright breaking openly into the most reactionary outburst that looks too much like a suppressed "real nature" struggling to come out, as for example, in the play by Tom Stoppard and Robert Bolt which attacked the October Revolution and justified it by vulgar statements like, "Leninism in action after 1917 was very much worse than anything which had gone in Tsarist Russia" (Stoppard) and that Lenin was "possessed by a terribly wrong idea" (Bolt).

Stoppard is a particularly instructive example not only because he puts the reactionary "case" so blatantly, but also because one suspects that he is saying things which many other alternative playwrights believe, but silently. Interviewed on the pages of the alternative theatre magazine, *Theatre Quarterly*, Stoppard has declared what amounts to a complete opposition to all kinds of political theatre, based on the rejection of 'all moralistic philosophy', and has come out with statements like: "There is a sense in which contradictory political arguments are restatements of each other. For example, Leninism and Fascism are restatement of totalitarianism,"[28] and "People tend to think of Stalinism as being something else, a perversion of Leninism. That is an absurd and foolish untruth, and it is one on which much of the Left bases itself. Lenin perverted Marxism and Stalin carried on."[29]

Now this sort of statement can be easily placed the context of Cold war propaganda, all the way from Orwell to Solzhenitsyn. It would seem, at least on the surface, to be in some kind of opposition to what the alternative theatre in Britain stands, or should stand, for. And yet, how is Stoppard's position different from that of the number one revolutionary playwright, Edward Bond, when he declares again in a *Theatre Quarterly* interview that:

> Lenin said we must have this elitist section to lead the party, because the proletariat just doesn't have enough consciousness to know what's going on. And Lenin of course went off his head—he was certainly round the bend when he died. So, when he died, Stalin could simply carry on—when you have an élite, you have to destroy the proletariat in some way.[30]

Or, when Bond accuses Brecht of being naïve because he would 'condemn the Nazis for doing things he is quite capable of praising the Communists for doing', he wants to say that the so-called doctrine of 'the end justifying the means' puts both in the same camp, which comes right out of the vulgar Cold War "theories" of "totalitarian" politics. It is significant that in that same interview and immediately following the question on Brecht, Bond expressed his deep admiration for Beckett adding, however, that 'it was wrong to make a cultural hero of him'. Presumably, such a position was "cut out" for Bond himself. The interview from which those statements came introduces him as 'a playwright and a prophet' who would give us his 'views on the human condition in technological society'.

Finally, there is David Edgar who is the typical representative of what may be called the alternative outlook—namely, a cluster of reactionary ideas constantly threatening to burst out of a pseudo-progressive shell. Significantly, Edgar, particularly after the success of his seemingly anti-fascist but actually pro-fascist play, *Destiny*, has taken on the task of summing up the experience of the movement, in an article titled "Ten Years of Political Theatre 1968–78" followed by a *Theatre Quarterly* interview.

To begin with, Edgar breaks not only with socialist realism, but with realism *tout court*. Admittedly, he also attacks naturalism, but for him the two are virtually indistinguishable. With dubious support from Brecht, whom he misunderstands, and from the pseudo-Marxist critic Terry Eagleton, he comes out openly for modernist styles like Dadaism and Expressionism as 'bolder and more aggressive' artistic tools. Next on the list is popular culture, which Edgar dismisses as useless, reactionary and atrophied. His argument is that because so much of the content of popular culture under capitalism is reactionary, the forms of that culture have been irredeemably infected, and, therefore, attempts by people like McGrath to 'inject socialist content into mass populist forms' are doomed to failure. Finally, having disposed of the realist and the popular forms, Edgar accomplishes his brilliant *coup d'etat* or *coup de theatre*, if you prefer, by the endorsement of none other than that despised form: bourgeois West End theatre. "It seems to me," he declares, "demonstrably if paradoxically true that the most potent, rich, and in many ways politically acute theatrical statements of the past ten years have been made in custom-built buildings patronized almost exclusively by the middle class."[31]

One strand in this kind of theatre which Edgar presents as particularly worthy of admiration is what he calls shock and disruption theatre. The plays, whether written by a Brenton or a Bond, which depend on their effect on shock, suspense, and "disruptive" violence, derive their esthetic, as Edgar admits, from the degenerate libertarian, anarchist and situationist tendencies of the early sixties. This esthetic could never by any stretch of the imagination be reconciled with socialism, to which it often is consciously opposed. Yet, Edgar concludes that the 'discoveries' of these writers are vital for socialist theatre and, in support of his argument, he quotes none other than Leon Trotsky about literature 'having its own laws' independent of those of politics, and about the 'sub-conscious process' of 'artistic creation'. With this kind of perspective the alternative theatre movement under the guidance of David Edgar can really move 'toward a theatre of dynamic ambiguities' (the title of his long *Theatre Quarterly* interview) except that the ambiguity is not merely dynamic (itself an ambiguous term), it is deeply damaging because it is the kind of ambiguity that confuses the progressive and the reactionary, the black and the white, the fascist and the ant-fascist.

· 6 ·

ISLAMOPHOBIA AND THE INTELLECTUALS

A well-known report from the Runnymede Trust in 1997 defined Islamophobia as "an outlook or world-view involving an unfounded dread and dislike of Muslims, which results in practices of exclusion and discrimination." Yet, although it is clear from this definition that Islamophobia is a form of racism, it has been adopted without embarrassment or secrecy by some who are considered to be intellectuals.

The British Columnist Polly Toynbee was one of the first such writers who declared openly nearly a decade ago in *The Independent* newspaper: "I am an Islamophobe." Similarly, Rod Liddle, writing for the *Sunday Times* had asked that he be "counted in" among the Islamophobes.

The most celebrated recent case of Islamophobia, however, remains that of the novelist, Martin Amis, who in an interview with *The Times* newspaper, declared that: "The Muslim community will have to suffer until it gets its house in order. Not letting them travel. Deportation; further down the road. Strip-searching people who look like they're from the Middle East or Pakistan. Discriminatory stuff, until it hurts the whole community and they start getting tough with their children."

It is to be expected that these declarations by Amis should create a stir in British intellectual circles which have come to reject such openly declared racist positions. It is also to be expected that other intellectuals and journalists should respond to him. What is surprising, however, is that another well-known novelist, Ian McEwan, has defended him and expressed views that are no less weird and racist than his.

In an interview with the Italian newspaper *Corriere della Sera*, McEwan, according to a report in the *Independent*, had said "I despise Islamism" because it wants "to create a society that I detest."

According to the British journalist, Peter Popham, who has published an article on this subject, McEwan's words could "lay him open to being investigated for a 'hate crime.'" According to the Italian newspaper, McEwan, who does not like interviews normally, consented to this interview to defend his "old friend", Martin Amis, who had been accused of racism because of his anti-Muslim remarks and because he shares those views with his friend.

It is worth recording that this cultural Islamophobia, if such racist remarks could be linked to culture at all, has not passed unnoticed by British intellectuals and writers themselves. In an article titled, "Fear of Islam: Britain's New Disease", published in the *Independent* last summer, and made into the basis for a film screened on channel 4 of British TV, "It shouldn't Happen to a Muslim", Peter Oborne proclaimed that "suspicion of the Muslim community has found its way into mainstream society – and nobody seems to care."

The truth of the matter is that opinions and arguments that are against racism and against Islamophobia, as a form of racism, whether cultural or religious, do not receive full support from the mainstream media nor from the powers that be which may well seek to encourage racist hatred as a way of controlling their populations and diverting their attention from the primary issues.

Any simple review of what has been written on this subject in the last few years will reveal the degree of the antipathy of the educated public opinion to Islamophobia, beginning with Juan Cole's presidential address to the Middle East Studies Association in 2006, titled "Islamophobia as a Social Problem", and passing through the five pages devoted to Islamophobia in Ali Rattansi's book on *Racism* in the Oxford very short introduction series in 2007, and ending in the first full-length book devoted to the subject, *Islamophobia: Making Muslims the Enemy* (2008), by Peter Gottschalk and Gabriel Greenberg. Significantly, two European conferences on the subject have also been held in recent years, "Racism, Postcolonialism, Europe" in the University of Leeds, 15–17 May, 2006, and "Antisemitism and Islamophobia in Europe", University College London, 22–24 June, 2008.

What is worthy of attention, as well as gratification, is that the awareness of the racism inherent in Islamophobia, whether in its European or its American form, has spread among the people and in the public opinion as well as among intellectuals.

In an article in the *Guardian*, titled "Demonstrators force far-right to halt launch of anti-Islam talks", Jess Smee reported on September 20, 2008, that "a far-right group was forced to abandon a press conference launching a campaign against plans for a new mosque and Muslim immigration in the German city of Cologne yesterday, when protesters targeted them with stones and paint. . . . Nearby around 500 of the protesters formed a human chain to defend the site where the city plans to build the mosque, Germany's largest . . . According to the organizers, the aim of the conference was to forge a "European, patriotic, populist rightwing movement" by uniting far-right speakers and supporters from across Europe. Among plans for yesterday was a tour of "multi-ethnic hotspots". . . . German government officials spoke out against the talks, saying it would be divisive for the city where more than a third of the 1 million residents are not German, but mostly of Turkish origin."

In fact, when the event did take place, it was attended by only 50 people when the organizers had expected 1500 people. Moreover, a very big counter-demonstration encircled the leaders of the right who had come by boat, threw stones at them and prevented them from landing. This was regarded as a great victory against the extreme right which received more than one slap in the face particularly when ordinary citizens also refused to have anything to do with them. Taxi drivers, it was reported, refused to take them away from where they were encircled. And police, too, refused for hours to help them leave the place.

One of the first writers to stand up to anti-Muslim and anti-Arab racism was Paul Kivel, who in an important early study titled *Uprooting Racism: How White People can Work for Racial Justice* (2002), had made these interesting remarks: "Such a climate of anti-Arab racism was much in evidence during the Gulf War against Iraq. For example, in a nationally televised briefing on NBC, February 27, 1991, General Norman Schwarzkopf, head of our military operations, stated that the Iraqis "are not part of the same human race as we are." *Time* magazine, the *New York Times*, and many other media carried editorials, articles, and cartoons describing Arabs as less than human . . . Arab Americans have reached the highest levels of professional achievement throughout the United States and Canada, have been political and social leaders, and have contributed to the arts and sciences. However, they continue to be vilified in the media, left out of mainstream political and social affairs, misrepresented in textbooks, and excluded from multicultural curricula. They are also readily blamed for the actions of Arabs and Muslims in any part of the world, and are vulnerable to verbal and physical attack simply for being of Arab descent . . . A final issue to consider is how anti-Arab racism allows us to be manipulated around foreign policy issues. In the last few years we have bombed Iraq, the Sudan, and Afghanistan, invaded Somalia, and supplied arms and other supplies to Israel . . . without a high level of anti-Arab feeling in the United States it would be impossible for our governments to justify destroying a civilian hospital in a foreign country (Sudan); invading and occupying a country we were not at war with (Somalia); maintaining a boycott of food and medical supplies that international observers report kill up to 5000 children a month (Iraq); or ignoring the occupation of, settlement in, and violence against the civilian population of yet another Arab country (Palestine)—all in clear breach of international law."

Four years later, during which period the racist anti-Muslim anti-Arab trend has strengthened, Juan Cole, as president of the Middle East Studies Association in the USA, in his "Islamophobia as a Social Problem" address, later published in the MSA bulletin in June 2007, bravely addressed the issue again and put it in its proper perspective: "Although a handful of the world's 1.3 billion Muslims have formed political and religious organizations that deploy terror as a tactic, it is a vanishingly small even if destructive minority. Nor is the adoption of this tactic confined to Muslims. In the 1970s, the German Baader Meinhoff Gang, the Japanese Red Army, the weathermen in the US, and the Irish Republican Army all used terror as a tactic and none was Muslim. Suicide bombing was pioneered not by Muslims but by the Tamil Tigers, leftists of Hindu heritage. In 1995—the Japan-based Om Shinrikyo let sarin gas loose in the Tokyo subway, hoping to kill thousands. They killed 12, but temporarily sickened thousands. Yet the American standup comedians do not make jokes about Japanese being terrorists, or about the Irish as terrorists, or about upper middle class anti-war white Americans as terrorists. They should not, of course, but it would not even occur to them that what they are doing is proactively marking Muslim as a distinctive social identity around which they are creating anxiety.

Timothy McVeigh would never be called a "white" terrorist, nor would it ever be intimated that whites have a tendency to terrorism. This is so in part because whiteness itself is a construct, one purpose of which is to create an unmarked identity with all its privileges."

Finally, it is important to point out the scholarly work that has come out in recent years on racism and on Islamophobia as a racist phenomenon, which unfortunately indicates the spread of this dangerous trend in the "advanced" western societies. Among these studies is Ali Rattansi's *Racism* (2007) mentioned earlier, which deals with contemporary as well as modern social and intellectual issues related to racism, and George M. Fredrickson's *Racism: A Short History* (2007) which deals with the new forms of racism and what he calls cultural racism as a new phenomenon in which, "the line between "culturalism" and racism is not difficult to cross. Culture and even religion can become essentialized to the point that they can serve as a functional equivalent of biological racism, as has to some extent occurred recently in the perception of blacks in the United States and Britain and of Muslims in several predominantly Christian nations."[1]

It is important, in conclusion, to point again to those western intellectuals who have openly stood against the racist Islamophobe trend in Britain and against writers like Martin Amis in particular. Among these Ronan Bennett stands out who in a brave article titled "Shame on Us" published on November 19, 2007, in *The Guardian*, declared that "Amis's views are symptomatic of a much wider and deeper hostility to Islam and intolerance of otherness . . . Amis should have been taken to task by his peers for his views. He was not . . ." He continues to explain that Amis's attempt to portray western societies as "more evolved" than Muslim societies is another clear racist formulation that contains echoes of the older anti-African, social-Darwinist, racism. He also uncovers the hypocrisy of those journalists who criticize Muslims for their Muslim schools while they "send their children to Christian or Jewish faith schools." He concludes that "this is a community under attack, and not just by novelists", and an environment has been created where we see "a major cultural and literary figure endorsing prejudice against Muslims." He concludes with these powerful words that contain a message to every British, American and western intellectual: "why did writers not start writing? There is Eagleton and there is the Indian novelist and essayist Pankaj Mishra, who took apart Amis's strange and chaotic essay on the sixth anniversary of 9/11. But where are the others? . . . I can't help feeling that Amis's remarks, his defense of them, and the reaction to them were a test. They were a test of our commitment to a society in which imaginative sympathy applies not just to those whose lives and beliefs run along different lines. And I can't help feeling we failed that test. Amis got away with it. He got away with as odious an outburst of racist sentiment as any public figure has made in this country for a very long time. Shame on him for saying it, and shame on us for tolerating it."

In an article, published in *The Guardian*, July 7, 2007, Terry Eagleton laments the fact that "British literature's long and rich tradition of politically engaged writers has come to an end" (the subtitle of the article), and locates a body of contemporary reactionary writing to which Martin Amis's racist remarks might be said to belong:

"The knighting of Salman Rushdie is the establishment's reward for a man who moved from being a remorseless satirist of the west to cheering on its criminal adventures in Iraq and Afghanistan. David Hare caved in to the blandishments of Buckingham Palace some years ago, moving from radical to reformist . . . Martin Amis has written of the need to prevent Muslims travelling and to strip-search people "who look like they're from the Middle East or from Pakistan." Deportation, he considers, may be essential further down the road."

Eagleton traces this trend back to the fifties, which he regards as the beginning of the end of a previous radical tradition in English literature. "In the postwar welfare state, however, the rot set in", he explains, "Philip Larkin, the period's unofficial poet laureate, was a racist, who wrote of stringing up strikers. Most of the Angry young Men of the 50s metamorphosed into Dyspeptic Old Buffers."

In the American context, the issue of Islamophobic racism made interesting dramatic appearances during the 2008 presidential campaign and Barack Obama's candidacy. Those events are too close to be forgotten, or to need any refreshing of the memory. The rampant racism openly expressed with regard to Obama being a closet Muslim and having an Arabic middle name was nauseating enough. One remembers the mind-boggling response of John McCain (when someone had protested that Obama was an Arab) that on the contrary he was a good family man. Remarks like these even forced such an establishment figure as Colin Powell to ask and since when has being a Muslim become a crime in the United States. The best intellectual response to this phenomenon, however, as our paper is about Islamophobia and the intellectuals, may be Naomi Klein's article, "Barack Obama ignores Islamophobia", published in *The Nation*, March 8, 2008, the concluding paragraph of which might be a suitable conclusion to this paper:

"As the most visible target of rising racism, Obama has the power to be more than its victim. He can use the attacks to begin the very process of global repair that is the most seductive promise of his campaign. The next time he's asked about his alleged Muslimness, Obama can respond not just by clarify-ing the facts but by turning the tables. He can state clearly that although a liaison with a pharmaceutical lobbyist may be worthy of scandalized exposure, being a Muslim is not. Changing the terms of the debate this way is not only morally just but tactically smart—it's the one response that could defuse these hateful attacks. The best part is this: unlike ending the Iraq War and closing Guantanamo, standing up to Islamophobia doesn't need to wait until after the election. Obama can use his campaign now. Let the repairing begin."

Among the repairing moves that should be taken to eliminate Islamophobia, one may mention the following measures: 1- Recognize Islamophobia as a form of racism and legislate against it by making it pun-ishable by law, like other forms of racism. 2- Speed up the entry of Muslim countries, like Turkey, into the EU, and make sure that they are not rejected on racist, Islamophobic grounds. 3- Legislate immediately against all forms of inciting hatred against Muslims and racism against Arabs. 4- Expose and publicize the cases of such Islamophobic anti-Arab racists as Kilroy-Silk, who said in an article in the Sunday Express, January 4, 2004: "We owe Arabs nothing", they have made no contribution to civilization. They have given us nothing, only "oil, suicide bombers, limb amputators and women oppressors." 5- And those mentioned in this paper, like Martin Amis, Polly Toynbee, and Ian McEwan. 6- And the Dutch, Geert Wilders, who, according to Taynor in the Observer, February 17, 2008, calls Islam "the ideology of a retarded culture" and says, "there can be no equality between our culture and the retarded Islamic culture", and concludes, "Islam is something we can't afford any more in the Netherlands. I want the fascist Koran banned. We need to stop the Islamisation of the Netherlands. That means no more mosques, no more Islamic schools, no more imams . . . Not all Muslims are terrorists, but almost all terrorists are Muslims." 7- Publicize the fact that in January, 2001, at the "Stockholm International Forum on Combating Intolerance", Islamophobia was recognized as a form of intolerance alongside Xenophobia and Anti-Semitism. 8- Put an end to the demonization of Islam and Muslims and expose the strategies of "humanitarian intervention" when they cover up new imperialist wars and adventures. 9- Expose Western cultural superior-ity, Eurocentric racism, and all forms of Western Exceptionalist discourse, for what they are, especially when they hide behind terms like "the Other", "Difference", "Multiculturalism", "Judeo-Christian Culture" (in deliberate exclusion of the Islamic component). 10- Explain that Islamophobia is not a spontaneous phenomenon, or one that merely reflects an aberrant aspect of human nature, but that it is a carefully orchestrated industry that serves the purposes of world domination by the big powers, and one that increasingly uses the forces of the extreme (fascist and racist) Right as its spearhead.

In fact, some may consider Obama's inauguration speech and, later, his speech in Cairo University, in June, 2009, as indications of a change in American (and consequently of generally Western) policy in this regard, signaling, perhaps, the end of Islamophobia. The reality, however, is more complex than that. The persistence, unfortunately, of Islamophobia may be seen in the repeated racist attacks, even if still confined to individual cases, and the continued stream of Islamophobic writing.

One of the examples of the latter may be the book, *America Alone*, by the Canadian writer, Mark Steyn, which has sold widely, and which contains, in addition to the usual Islamophobic declarations, the unabashed call for United States superiority and hegemony. Ideas similar to these are also spread by the British historian, Niall Ferguson, the American diplomat, Timothy Savage, in addition to the British novelist, Marin Amis, the American commentator, Daniel Pipes, and the political leaders of the European extreme Right.

Lately, Kanan Malik has exposed in detail, in a new article published in the magazine, *New Humanist*, May-June, 2009, the recent writings that propagate the fear of the spread of Islam in Europe and of the expected numerical domination of Muslims in the coming decades, and has connected these kinds of writing with their Islamophobic roots in the works of people like Martin Amis, Samuel Huntington, and Bernard Lewis. A similar refutation of these alarmist, Islamophobic views has appeared in the cover article of *Newsweek*, 20 July, 2009, written by William Underhill, under the title of "The Myth of Eurabia: The False Fears of A Muslim Takeover" or "Why the fears of Islamic domination are all wrong: Analyzing the forecasts of an emerging 'Eurabia', hostile to America and western values."

RADICALS, RENEGADES, PUNDITS AND IMPOSTERS: REFLECTIONS ON THE INTERNATIONAL INTELLIGENTSIA

I

Since the end of the Second World War, there developed in the West a phenomenon best named the international intelligentsia that consisted of a number of prominent intellectuals, who represented a sort of "conscience of the West", and by extension of the world at large.

During the Vietnam War era, the two figures most exemplary of this group were Bertrand Russell and Jean-Paul Sartre. These intellectuals helped to remove borders and barriers between states, nations, and peoples, to become, in effect, spokesmen for all of humanity.

By contrast, the figures who stood out most prominently among the intelligentsia in the previous era were writers like George Orwell and Arthur Koestler, who had defected from the Left and were "recruited" for Cold War services.

In the contemporary era of globalism and so-called postcolonialism, similar groups and trends may be identified. The first may be called the radicals, represented most obviously by figures like Noam Chomsky, who continued, in their own way, the kind of radical critique of western imperialist politics carried on during the sixties and the seventies by thinkers like Sartre and Russell.

Their efforts, despite their limitations, nominate them for a place among the international intelligentsia as spokesmen for the interests of humanity at large.

In contrast, there is a second group of intellectuals that has roots in the Third World, but has turned against it. They can be compared to figures of the previous era, like Orwell, Koestler, and others, who had roots in the left, but turned against it and were used for purposes of Cold War propaganda. In the globalist era where any move toward independence , whether political, economic, or cultural, from the grips of imperialism is portrayed as the barbaric antagonist that has to be defeated (a place reserved for communism back in the Cold War era) these writers continue the older tradition of the renegades and turn-coats of that period.

Another group, whom I would call the pundits, represented by figures like Samuel Huntington and Thomas Friedman, speak for imperialist interests and are supported financially, and politically, by them. Instead of helping to remove walls and barriers between peoples, these figures, on the contrary, help to create tensions and divisions in the world. Due to their prominence in the media, these figures have become internationalized. They are indeed international rogue figures and voices that advocate war, conflict, imperialist exploitation and racist superiority that divide the world and enslave humanity.

The impressive collection of essays, *Why America's Top Pundits are Wrong* (2005), may well be the first comprehensive challenge and refutation of such pundits, exemplified here by the four figures of Samuel Huntington, Thomas L. Friedman, Robert Kaplan, and Dinesh D'Souza. The editors of this courageous work characterize the writings of these pundits as a set of reactionary myths that relentlessly poison American public discourse, such as "that conflict between people of different cultures, races, or genders is inevitable; that biology is destiny; that culture is immutable; that terrible poverty, inequality, and suffering are natural; and that people in other societies who do not want to live just like Americans are afraid of "modernity.""[1] They continue, explaining the damage brought about by these pundits and the justification for exposing them: "Often based on stereotypes of other people, these myths hobble our ability to think critically or to empathize with different kinds of people, and they have the effect of legitimating the status quo. They are also based on wrongheaded assumptions about human nature that we are determined to debunk."[2]

The editors of the volume conclude by summing up the position of these pundits and their own counter-response in this way: "The pundits critiqued in this book all share what we might call a reactionary determinism . . . If

African Americans are disproportionately poor, it is because they are intellectually inferior, and social programs cannot change this; the rape of women is an inevitable consequence of our genes, not the result of a distorted culture; globalization is in the hands of "the electronic herd" and cannot be remade in a more humane fashion by activists, trade unionists, and environmentalists; the Serbs, Croats, and Muslims will keep on killing one another because that is the way they are; democracy will not come to Asia because it does not fit their timeless culture; and people from different cultural traditions are destined to interact antagonistically rather that constructively. The authors of this book, believing that these ideas are based not only on bad politics but also on bad social science, promote a kind of realism different from that espoused by the pundits . . . While the pundits whisper in our ears that nothing can be done to make the world a better place, we know that this is wrong."[3]

More specifically on Huntington, the book points out that "Huntington's characterizations of different cultures are often based on egregious stereotypes (Muslims are violent fundamentalists, the Chinese are authoritarian) that blur the diversity of opinion and belief within a society and deny the ability of societies to change over time."[4] Similarly, Thomas L. Friedman's triumphalist defense of Globalism is sharply criticized, particularly in his presentation of Globalism as an uncontrollable panacea for all the problems of the world, and his perception of a global clash between what he calls modernity (associated only with the West) and tradition (associated largely with the "rest") that he sees as the cause of all conflicts.

Yet another group of intellectuals, whom one may call imposters, have been ably, and entertainingly, exposed by Alan Sokal and Jean Bricmont in their book entitled, *Fashionable Nonsense: Postmodern Intellectuals' Abuse of Science* (Picador—New York, 1998), and first published in France as *Impostures Intellectuelles* by Editions Odile Jacob, 1997.

As the two authors explain in their preface, "The book grew out of the now-famous hoax in which one of us published, in the American cultural-studies journal *Social Text*, a parody article crammed with nonsensical, but unfortunately authentic, quotations about physics and mathematics by prominent French and American intellectuals: Alan Sokal, "Transgressing the boundaries: Towards a transformative hermeneutics of quantum gravity." (1996)[5]

The purpose of the hoax was to show that "famous intellectuals such as Lacan, Kristeva, Isigaray, Baudrillard, and Deleuze" are basically charlatans who have abused scientific concepts and terminology and thrown around scientific jargon to impress "their non-scientific readers" without any regard for "its relevance or meaning."[6] Further on, Sokal explains more sharply that "they imagine, perhaps, that they can exploit the prestige of the natural sciences in order to give their own discourse a veneer of rigor. And they seem confident that no one will notice their misuse of scientific concepts. No one is going to cry out that the king is naked. Our goal is precisely to say that the king is naked (and the queen too)."[7]

Sokal's article is built on an extreme form of cognitive relativism, fashionable among certain French and American intellectuals, condemned later in the book as imposters, whose claim to fame is that it has challenged the old "dogma" that "there exists an external world, whose properties are independent of any individual human being and indeed of humanity as a whole", and has "proclaimed categorically that 'physical reality', no less than social 'reality' is at bottom a social and logistic construct." And by a series of unbelievable illogicalities, has arrived at the conclusion that "the pie of Euclid and the G of Newton, formerly thought to be constant and universal, are now perceived in their ineluctable historicity; and the putative observer becomes fatally decentered, disconnected from any epistemic link to a space-time point that can no longer be defined by geometry alone."[8]

And yet the article was published. Adding insult to injury, and in a totally self-defeating manner, as the authors explain, "it was published in a special issue of *Social Text* devoted to rebutting the criticisms leveled against postmodernism and social constructivism by several distinguished scientists. For the editors of *Social Text*, it was hard to imagine a more radical way of shooting themselves in the foot."[9]

When the hoax was revealed, the scandal hit the front pages of the *New York Times*, *The International Herald Tribune*, *The Observer* and *Le Monde*, as the authors exposed formed a "veritable pantheon" of contemporary French theoreticians such as Gilles Deleuze, Jacques Derrida, Felix Guattari, Luce Irigaray, Jacques Lacan, Bruno Latour, Jean-Francois Lyotard, Michel Serres, and Paul Virilio, to whom many prominent American academics were added.[10]

Many researchers in the humanities and social sciences wrote to Sokal in support of his exposé and in indignation at the charlatanism of the intellectual imposters. Sokal, himself, later wrote in his book justifying why he did what he did: "But why did I do it [write that hoax article]? I confess that I'm an unabashed Old Leftist who never quite understood how deconstruction was supposed to help the working class. And I'm a stodgy old scientist who believes, naively, that there exists an external world, that there exist objective truths about that world, and that my job is to discuss some of them. (If science were merely a negotiation of social conventions about what is agreed to be "true", why should I bother devoting a large fraction of my all-too-short life to its?[11])

This conscious purpose of correcting something the authors felt was terribly wrong with the intellectual scene in France (and in the West generally) and of exposing the great hoax that they felt is played on the public by these 'intellectual imposters' is explained clearly and openly by Sokal and Bricmont, both of whom are natural scientists, who could not be fooled by such abuse of science and scientific concepts:

"A second target of our book is epistemic relativism, namely the idea— which, at least when expressed explicitly, is much more widespread in the English speaking world than in France—that modern science is nothing more than a "myth", a "narration" or a "social construction" among many others."[12]

"This book deals with mystification, deliberately obscure language, confused thinking, and the misuse of scientific concepts."[13]

"Our aim is, quite simply, to denounce intellectual posturing and dishonesty, from wherever they come. If a significant part of the postmodernist "discourse" in contemporary American and British academia is of French origin, it is equally true that English language intellectuals have long since given it an authentic home-grown flavor."[14]

"The main problem raised by these texts is that she [Julia Kristera] makes no effort to justify the relevance of these mathematical concepts to the fields she is purporting to study–linguistics, literary criticism, political philosophy, psychoanalysis—and this, in our opinion, is for the very good reason that there is none. Her sentences are more meaningful than those of Lacan, but she surpasses even him for the superficiality of her erudition."[15]

"Postmodernism has three principal negative effects: a waste of time in the human sciences, a cultural confusion that favors obscurantism, and a weakening of the political left."[16]

"The Lakadaisical attitude toward scientific rigor that one finds in Lacan, Kristeva, Beaudrillard, and Deleuze had an undeniable success in France during the 1970's and is still remarkably influential there. This way of thinking spread outside France, notably in the English-speaking world, during the 1980's and 1990's."[17]

In support of their argument about the serious damage brought about by postmodernist relativism on the social sciences, the authors quote Eric Hobsbawm, who has cautioned against: "The rise of "postmodernist" intellectual fashions in Western universities, particularly in departments of literature and anthropology, which imply that all "facts" claiming objective existence are simply intellectual constructions. In short, that there is no clear distinction between fact and fiction."[18]

The book ends eloquently with an explanation of the political damage of postmodernism and with the hope for the emergence of an intellectual culture that would replace it: "Finally, for all those of us who identify with the political left, postmodernism has specific negative consequences. First of all, the extreme focus on language and the elitism linked to the use of a pretentious jargon contribute to enclosing intellectuals in sterile debates and to isolating them from social movements taking place outside their ivory tower."[19]

"If all discourses are merely "stories" or "narratives", and none is more objective or truthful than another, then one must concede that the worst sexist or raciest prejudices and the most reactionary socio-economic theories are "equally valid", at least as descriptions or analyses of the real world (assuming that one admits the existence of a real world). Clearly, relativism is an extremely weak foundation on which to build a criticism of the existing social order."[20]

"Our hopes, [for after postmodernism] however, go in a different direction: the emergence of an intellectual culture that would be rationalist but not dogmatic, scientifically minded but not scientistic, open-minded but not frivolous, and politically progressive but not sectarian. But this, of course, is only a hope, and perhaps only a dream."[21]

II

Edward Said's 1993 Reith Lectures, *Representations of the Intellectual*, published by Pantheon Books, Random House, 1994 and Vintage Books, NY, 1996, is also important in this context, on the question of intellectuals generally, as well as on the question of the Arab intellectual (written as it was in the same period as books by Makiya, *Cruelty and Silence* (1993), and Ajami, *The Dream Palace of the Arabs* (1998), to which the last pages of the book are a kind of reply 117–121). These are six lectures titled: 1. Representations of the Intellectual, 2. Holding Nations and Traditions at Bay, 3. Intellectual Exile: Expatriates and Marginals, 4. Professionals and Amateurs, 5. Speaking Truth to Power, and 6. Gods that Always Fail.

In spite of the repetition of typical Saidian themes and typical Saidian ways of "being wrong", this booklet is important both for the topic of intellectuals and for the limited theme of the Arab intellectual. It also contains some positive statements in addition to the many "wrong" formulations that are also important for the way they teach by "negative example", again as typical of Said.

Said mentions, in his "Introduction", John Carey's "interesting book" (his description), *The Intellectuals and the Masses,* and says "I found its on the whole dispiriting findings complementary to mine."[22] While it is a positive sign for Said to single out this particular book for praise, which it wholly deserves, his choice of adjectives is indicative. The book is more than just the neutral "interesting"—it is, in fact, unique in the way it counters most of dominant and current Anglo-Saxon criticism. Secondly, the choice of "dispiriting" to describe the book's "findings" is highly unusual. Why "dispiriting" and dispiriting for who? I found it, on the contrary, quite uplifting in the way it explored reactionary and proto-fascist intellectuals, only for whom and for their followers or sympathizers could the book be called "dispiriting". Finally, there is not much in common between Carey's book and the topics addressed by Said or, more importantly, his perspective on them.

In the same introduction, Said says: "There can be little doubt that figures like James Baldwin and Malcolm X define the kind of work that has most influenced my own representations of the intellectual's consciousness"[23] without explaining the nature of this influence or the points of similarity.

Similarly, his rejection of Fukuyama, Lyotard and Huntington is done rather briefly and mildly, like his endorsement of "such celebrated and energetic dissenters as Noam Chomskyy or Gore Vidal", in the same "Introduction."[24]

The second lecture, "Holding Nations and Traditions at Bay", for example, which has interesting and positive statements like:

Things have changed a great deal since then [Julien Benda's, *The Treason of Intellectuals* of 1927 with which the first lecture had started]. In the first place, Europe and the West are no longer the unchallenged standard for the rest of the world.[25]

During the Gulf War public discussion of the crisis, especially on television but also in print journalism, assumed the existence of this national "we", which was repeated by reporters, military personnel, and ordinary citizens alike, such as "when are *we* going to begin the ground war," or "have *we* incurred any casualties?"[26]

How difficult it was during the recent Gulf War against Iraq to remind citizens that the U.S. was not an innocent or disinterested power (the invasions of Vietnam and Panama were conveniently forgotten by policy-makers), nor was it appointed by anyone except itself as the world's policeman.[27]

> All this is part of maintaining a national identity. To feel, for example, that the
> Russians are coming, or that the Japanese economic invasion is upon us, or that
> militant Islam is on the march, is not only to experience collective alarm, but also to
> consolidate "our" identity as beleaguered and at risk.[28]

While Said accurately points to Noam Chomsky and Gore Vidal as the
two key intellectuals in the U.S., who have questioned this manufactured,
consensual identity, he reveals his ignorance of other traditions when he
singles out "intellectuals like Ali Shariati, Adonis, Kamal Abu Deeb, the
intellectuals of the May 4th Movement [who] provocatively disturb the mon-
umental calm and inviolate aloofness of the tradition" in "cultures like the
Islamic or the Chinese, with their fabulous continuities and immensely secure
basic symbols."[29]

Why those three figures particularly? And why refer to a movement that
goes back to 1919 (no matter how important!), and what exactly is implied by
"their fabulous continuities and immensely secure basic symbols"?

Lecture 3, "Intellectual Exile, Expatriates and Marginals", is particularly
weak in the way it lumps together widely divergent and incongruous figures
under the inadequate term of exile, figures that range from Ovid, to V.S.
Naipaul, to Thomas Mann, to Jonathan Swift, to Adonis, to C.L.R. James. At
some point, even Henry Kissinger and Zbigniew Brzezinski are briefly included
among the exiles [hopefully not among the intellectuals!].

The figure who stands out for Said and who receives the longest coverage
is Adorno, whom Said describes thus:

> Even more rigorous, more determinedly the exile than Naipaul, is Theodore
> Wiesengrund Adorno. He was a forbidding but endlessly fascinating man, and for
> me, the dominating intellectual conscience of the middle twentieth century, whose
> entire career skirted and fought the dangers of fascism, communism and Western
> consumerism.[30]

Putting fascism, communism, and capitalism in one boat is surely indicative. So is the laudatory reference to the reactionary figure of Naipaul. Said
strongly endorses Adorno's dubious conclusion: "For him life was at its most fake
in the aggregate—the whole is always the untrue, he once said—and this, he
continued, placed an even greater premium on subjectivity, on the individual's
consciousness, on what could not be regimented in the totally administered society,"[31] which is blatant bourgeois individualism. Said continues: "Adorno was the
quintessential intellectual, hating *all* systems, whether on our side or theirs, with
equal distaste."[32] He singles out for praise one fragment, number 18, in *Minima*

Moralia ("published in 1953, and subtitled "Reflection from a Damaged Life"), because, according to Said, it captures the significance of exile quite perfectly. "Dwelling, in the proper sense," says Adorno, "is now impossible. The traditional residences we have grown up in have grown intolerable: each trait of comfort is paid for with a betrayal of knowledge, each vestige of shelter with the musty part of family interests . . . *It is part of morality not to be at home in one's home*,"[33] which are strange words, indeed, to be admired by a spokesman for Palestinians, the exemplary "homeless" people of the 20th century.

This limited, indeed inescapably bourgeois, perspective of Said on the question of "exile" appears further on, when he says:

> So while it is true to say that exile is the condition that characterizes the intellectual as someone who stands as a marginal figure outside the comforts of privilege, power, being-at-homeless (so to speak), it is also very important to stress that that condition carries with it certain rewards and, yes, even privileges. So while you are neither winning prizes nor being welcomed into all those self-congratulating honor societies that routinely exclude embarrassing troublemakers who do not toe the party line, you *are* at the same time deriving some positive things from exile and marginality.[34]

The fifth lecture, "Speaking Truth to Power", although seemingly straightforward in its main thesis, also does not lack its problems. For example, Said seems to endorse Focault's and Barthes's death of the author thesis. "There has even been an influential school of philosophers, among whom Michel Foucault ranks very high, who say that to speak of an author at all (as in "the author of Milton's poems") is a highly tendentious, not to say ideological, overstatement."[35] And:

> I think it is true to say that the critique of objectivity and authority did perform a positive service by underlining how, in the secular world, human beings construct their truths, and that, for example, the so-called objective truth of the white Man's superiority built and maintained by the classical European colonial empires also rested on a violent subjugation of African and Asian peoples, who, it is equally true, fought that particular improved "truth" in order to provide an independent order of their own. And so now everyone comes forward with new and often violently opposed views of the world: one hears endless talk about Judeo-Christian values, Afrocentric values, Muslim truths, Eastern truths, Western truths, each providing a complete program excluding all the others.[36]

Isn't this the infamous "Clash of Civilizations" thesis expressed in different words? And the conclusion is anti-universalist: "The result is an almost complete absence of universals, even though very often the rhetoric suggests, for instance, that "our" values (whatever those may happen to be) are in fact universal."[37]

The last lecture, "Gods that Always Fail", is also fraught with its own particular contradictions. Examples:

> For fourteen years I served as an independent member of the Palestinian parliament in exile, the Palestine National Council, the total number of whose meetings in so far as I attended them at all amounted to about a week altogether.[38]

> I do not want to equivocate or allow myself very much ambiguity at the outset. I am against conversion to and belief in a political God of any sort.[39]

The phrase "political God" is derived from the title of Richard Crossman's book *The God that Failed* (1949). Said's account of the book and the episodes in Cold War history that it refers to, although he does seem to reject what he calls Crossman's "emphatically theological terms", is oddly positive:

> Intended as a testimonial to the gullibility of prominent Western intellectuals who included Ignazio Silone, Andre Gide, Arthur Koestler, and Stephen Spender among others—*The God that Failed* allowed each of them to recount his experiences of the road to Moscow, the inevitable disenchantment that followed, the subsequent re-embrace of non-Communist faith.[40]

Said's conclusion, paradoxically, is no different from the Cold War conclusion of the book itself:

> The battle for the intellect has been transformed into a battle for the soul, with implications for intellectual life that have been very baleful. That was certainly the case in the Soviet Union and its satellites, where show trials, mass purges, and a gigantic penitentiary system exemplified the horrors of the ordeal on the other side of the iron curtain.[41]

The whole issue, Said seems to say, was trivial as those intellectuals' original belief in Marxism was unacceptable:

> To read over *The God That Failed* testimonial is for me a depressing thing. I want to ask: Why as an intellectual did you believe in a God anyway? And besides, who gave you the right to imagine that your early belief and later disenchantment were so important?[42]

This is both *naïve* (for not understanding or wanting to understand the importance of this book for Cold War propaganda purposes) and, more damagingly, *supportive* of this very Cold War ideology the book is meant to serve (in accepting the phrase and the thesis of the book that being a communist or a Marxist was like believing blindly in a God).

III

Two books that mark the beginning and the current terminal point in the study of "renegade intellectuals" , as well as of a whole epoch of Western intellectual history, are *The God that Failed* (1950), edited by Richard H. Crossman (reprinted by the Columbia University Press—New York, 2001) and *Who Paid the Piper?* by Frances Stonor Saunders reprinted as *The Cultural Cold War: The CIA and the World of Arts and Letters* (The New Press—New York, 1999).

The God that Failed is based on biographical experiences of six writers divided into two groups, described as "the Initiates", who include Arthur Koestler, Ignazio Silone and Richard Wright, and the "worshippers from afar", Andre Gide, Louis Fischer, and Stephen Spender. As Crossman says in his introduction to the book, "In this book, six intellectuals describe their journey into Communism and the return."[43]

While Crossman admits that "the only link, indeed, between these six very different personalities is that all of them—after tortured struggles of conscience—chose Communism because they had lost faith in democracy and were willing to sacrifice "bourgeois liberties in order to defeat fascism,"[44] and convincingly concludes that "the intellectual attraction of Marxism was that it exploded liberal fallacies—which really were fallacies. It taught the bitter truth that progress is not automatic, that boom and slump are inherent in capitalism, that social injustice and racial discrimination are not cured merely by the passage of time, and that power politics cannot be "abolished", but only used for good or bad ends,"[45] he descends into what we nowadays call "orientalist discourse", inevitably masking a racist belief in the inherent superiority of the "West" to the "East", and its political expression in this case as the superiority of "Western democracy" to "Russian (i.e. oriental) Communism":

> But it is clear that, as soon as the intellectual convert began to know more about conditions in Russia, his mood changed. Humility was replaced—and Silone describes this very clearly—by a belief (for which Marx, who had an utter contempt for the Slavs, gave plenty of authority) that the West must bring Enlightenment to

the proletariat. This belief was both the beginning of disillusionment and an excuse for remaining in the Party. Disillusionment, because the main motive for conversion had been despair of Western civilization, which was now found to contain values essential for the redemption of Russian Communism; and excuse, because it could be argued that if the Western influence were withdrawn, Oriental brutality would turn the defense of human freedom into loathsome tyranny.[46]

Crossman degenerates further into open racism when he describes Richard Wright in this way: "As an American Negro, Wright both belongs and does not belong to Western democracy."[47]

Crossman, as a spokesman for British social-imperialism, cannot hide his allegiance and his imperialist/racist perspective on the events of the 20th century (such key events as the Indian Independence, the triumph of the Chinese Revolution and the rising tide of the national liberation movements all over Africa and the Third World that occurred precisely in the years of surrounding the publication of this book) as can be seen in his continuing argument on the topic of Richard Wright:

It was as an American writer, imbued with a Western sense of human dignity and artistic values, that he fell foul of the Communist apparatus. But as a Negro, he utters that tragic sentence after he has left the Party. "I'll be for them, even if they are not for me." Millions of colored people are not subjected to the complex conflict through which Richard Wright paused. For them Western democracy still means simply "white ascendancy." Outside the Indian subcontinent, where equality has been achieved through a unique act of Western statesmanship, Communism is still a gospel of liberation among the Colored peoples; and the Chinese or African intellectual can accept it as such without destroying one half of his personality.[48]

The Foreword to the 2001 edition of *The God that Failed*, provided by David C. Engerman, a professor at the Department of History, in Brandeis University, clearly explains the utilization of this book and the six figures contained in it for the purposes of the Cold War in association also with such organizations as the CIA-Sponsored Congress for Cultural Freedom (CCF) and Journals like the British *Encounter*, the Italian *Tempo Presente* and the French *Preuves*.

Engerman sums up his Foreword thus:

The publication history of the book makes this last point [its role in the cultural Cold War] clear. Not only was the book widely distributed through CCF channels—and thus purchased with CIA funds—but both the American and the British occupation forces in Germany used the book there. By 1952, the newly formed United States Information Service held all foreign rights to the book. The republication of the book in the 1980's suggests another element of the intellectual transformation. In 1983,

three years after the election of Ronald Reagan as President, the last Cold-War edition of the book appeared, this time published by Henry Regnery Publishers, which
bills itself as "America's most dedicated conservative publisher." Perhaps, with this
first post-Cold War edition, we can return to the book for an education in the history
of the Cold War as well as in the responsibilities of intellectuals.[49]

The cultural aspects of this history is described and elucidated over more
than four hundred pages in Frances Stonor Saunders's still unsurpassed: *The
Cultural Cold War: The CIA and the World of Arts and Letters* (New Press- NY,
1999). In an illumining remark, Saunders aptly describes this grand policy in
which *The God that Failed* played a prominent part:

> Indeed, for the CIA, the strategy of promoting the Non-Communist Left was to
> become 'the theoretical foundation of the Agency's political operations against
> Communism over the next two decades.' The ideological rationale for this strategy in
> which the CIA achieved a convergence, even an identity, with leftist intellectuals,
> was presented by Schlesinger in *The Vital Center*, one of these seminal books which
> appeared in 1949 (the other two being *The God that Failed*, and Orwell's *Nineteen
> Eighty-Four*).[50]

Some of the interesting items in Saunders's book are her remark that "the
New York Times alleged in 1977 that the CIA had been involved in the publication of at least a thousand books."[51] And her remarks on the writer as spy:
"The phenomenon of writer as spy, spy as writer, was by no means new." She
singles out Somerset Maugham (whose "collection of Autobiographic stories,
Ashenden, was a bible for intelligence officers"), Compton Mackenzie, who
"worked for MI5 in the 1930's and Graham Greene who was "an undercover
agent for MI5 during—and, it is said, after—the Second World War."[52]

One of the rare continuations of the study of intellectuals, power and politics into the "post-Cold War" era is Mark Lilla's *The Reckless Mind: Intellectuals
in Politics* (New York Review Books—New York, 2001), which devotes its
chapters to modern and contemporary intellectuals, in this way: chapter 1,
Martin Heidegger, Hannah Arendt and Karl Jaspers, chapter 2, Carl Schmidt,
Chapter 3, Walter Benjamin, Chapter 4, Alexander Kojeve, Chapter 5, Michel
Foucault and Chapter 6, Jacques Derrida.

The book illuminates, for example, Walter Benjamin's paradoxical oscillation between Zionism and Marxism, when it explains that Benjamin

> Like many German Jews drawn to the early essays of Martin Buber, flirted with politi-
> cal Zionism in the summer of 1912. But in a letter to his friend Ludwig Strauss later
> that September, he wrote "I see three Zionist forms of Jewishness: Palestine Zionism

(a natural necessity); Germen Zionism in its halfness; and cultural Zionism, which sees Jewish values *everywhere* and works for them. Here I will stay, and I believe I must stay." This would remain his position throughout his life."[53]

and Marxism: "Those who knew Walter Benjamin recognized that he underwent a conversion (his word) from theological speculation to Marxism in the later 1920s, although neither they nor his later readers ever agreed on what that conversion meant."[54] It elaborates:

> In May 1925 Benjamin wrote to Scholem that if his current publishing plans did not work out, "I will probably hasten my involvement with Marxist politics and join the Party"—though he was also toying with the idea of learning Hebrew instead; soon afterward he wrote to Martin Buber that he was being torn between "cultic and communist activity."[55]

The book is also illuminating on Michel Foucault's political turning (s)—from a disciple of Nietzsche ("It was understood in France that Foucault was not a strict Marxist like Althusser, that he considered himself a disciple of Nietzsche, but it was assumed he shared the pacific and libertarian assumptions of the radical left he embraced",[56]) to a supporter of the Maoist *Gauche Proletarienne* in the early seventies and an advocate of "acts of justice by the people,"[57] to an admirer of the anti-Marxist so-called New Philosophers of France, as announced in the book, *The Marxist Thinkers* (1977), by the former Maoist Andre Glucksmann, which was given "a rave review" by Focault, as well as of the more traditional rightist figures like Friedrich A. Hayek and Ludwig von Mises.[58]

Derrida's paradoxical and ultimately nonsensical association with both Marxism and Deconstruction is also lucidly discussed.[59]

Among the renegade intellectuals, one may include Paul Johnson, a former editor of the "Left" British journal, *The New Statesman*, who wrote a book, *Intellectuals* (Weidenfeld and Nicolson—London, 1988), which aimed to be "an examination of the moral and judgmental credentials of certain leading intellectuals to give advice to humanity on how to conduct its affairs."[60] These intellectuals turn out to be Rousseau, Shelley, and Karl Marx to start with, then passing through Ibsen and Tolstoy to such 20th century figures as Ernest Hemingway, Bertolt Brecht, Bertrand Russell and Jean-Paul Sartre, to end with the contemporary figure of Noam Chomsky. The book could easily have been written to demonstrate (and, in fact, does demonstrate in spite of its declared aim) the originality of these intellectuals and their enormous influence on people's minds, as well as on the subsequent course of events. In fact, the book argues against itself from its very first paragraph and throughout:

> Over the past two hundred years the influence of intellectuals has grown steadily. Indeed, the rise of the secular intellectual has been a key factor in shaping the modern world. Seen against the long perspective of history it is in many ways a new phenomenon. It is true that in their earlier incarnations as priests, scribes and soothsayers, intellectuals have laid claim to guide society from the very beginning. But as guardians of hieratic cultures, whether primitive or sophisticated, their moral and ideological innovations were limited by the canons of external authority and by the inheritance of tradition. They were not, and could not be, free spirits, adventurers of the mind.[61]

Notice how the condemnation implied in the last two sentences is contradicted by the judgment of the first two.

Another example of the modern (or contemporary) renegade is David Horowitz. Regarded once as one of the founders of the American New Left in the sixties, who wrote such books that exposed U.S. imperialism as *Free World Colossus: A Critique of American Foreign Policy in the Cold War* (1965), he has turned 180 degrees and has come to write books like *The Politics of Bad Faith: The Radical Assault on America's Future* (1998), *Left Illusions: An Intellectual Odyssey* (2003), *Unholy Alliance: Radical Islam and the American Left* (2004), *The Professors: The 101 Most Dangerous Academics in America* (2006), *The Party of Defeat: How Democrats and Radicals Undermine America's War on Terror before and after 9–11* (2008), and *One-Party Classroom: How Radical Professors at America's Top Colleges Indoctrinate Students and Undermine our Democracy* (2000), and to organize meetings and conferences against what he calls "Islamofascism" in American Universities. Born again as a latter-day McCarthyite, he includes in his list of the 101 "most dangerous" professors such renowned writers and academics as Noam Chomsky, Juan Cole, John Esposito, Amiri Baraka, Norman Finkelstien, Todd Gitlin, bell hooks, Frederic Jameson, Howard Zinn, and many others.

An appropriate conclusion to our discussion of the figure of the renegade may well be its contemporary embodiment in Christopher Hitchens. A former Trotskyist, who wrote for the British weekly, *The New Statesman*, and who was brave enough to expose such Western leaders and venerated symbols as, among the most prominent, Bill Clinton (in a full-length book entitled, *No one Left to Lie to*) and Henry Kissinger (in another full-length book entitled, *The Trial of Henry Kissinger*), as well as mother Teresa (in yet another full-length book, entitled *The Missionary Position*) and the British royal family, but who turned into a drum-beater for the American wars on Iraq and Afghanistan and an outspoken Islamophobe.

Hitchens minces no words when it comes to religion, but it is clear that his "radical atheism" becomes merely a cover for the political aims of his Islamophobia. Thus, he declares openly: "The cause of backwardness and misery in the Muslim world is not Western oppression but Islam itself, a faith that promulgates contempt for Enlightenment and secular values. It teaches hatred to children, promises a grotesque version of an afterlife, elevates the cult of "martyrdom", flirts with the mad idea of the forced conversion of the non-Islamic world, and deprives societies of talents and energies of 50 percent of their members: the female half."[62]

This comes from the "Foreword" that Hitchens wrote for *Infidel*, the biographical work of Ayaan Hirsi Ali, who is also a Third World kind of renegade, who, like Salman Rushdie and others, deliberately exploit their anti-Islamism to gain fame and privilege in the West and who usually end up siding with its most reactionary political elements. In her most recent work, Ali comes up with such gems as: "Muslim children all over the world are taught the way I was, taught to perpetrate violence, taught to wish for violence against the infidel, the Jew, the American Satan,"[63] and "The Muslim mind needs to be opened. Above all, the uncritical Muslim attitude toward the Quran urgently needs to change, for it is a direct threat to peace. Today 1.57 billion people identify themselves as Muslims. Although they certainly have 1.57 billion different minds, they share a dominant cultural trend: The Muslim mind today seems to be in the grip of Jihad,"[64] and "All human beings are equal, but all cultures and religions are not . . . It is part of Muslim culture to oppress women and part of all tribal cultures to institutionalize patronage, nepotism, and corruption. The culture of the Western Enlightenment is better,"[65] and, finally, "there is beautiful architecture, yes, and encouragement of charity, yes, but Islam is built on sexual inequality and on the surrender of individual responsibility and choice. This is not just ugly; it is monstrous."[66]

· 8 ·

POWER AND THE RADICAL ARAB INTELLECTUAL: THREE CASE STUDIES

This chapter attempts to analyze the complexities of the relationship between the radical, Arab intellectual and political power in modern times through the examination of three cases—those of Taha Hussain, Al-Jawahiry, and Edward Said. Spanning the course of the whole of the twentieth-century, the careers of these three key, radical Arab intellectuals offer illustrative and illuminating examples of the relationship between political power and intellectuals in the Arab world generally. Although there are important differences between the three key figures—with Taha Hussain being the major example of the pioneering Arab intellectual of the early decades of the twentieth-century, the period of the Arab intellectual awakening, Al-Jawahiry, the exemplary political poet and intellectual and key leader in a mass political movement, and Edward Said, the exemplary Arab radical intellectual in exile who achieved international prestige and prominence—they share particularly illuminating similarities in the way they dealt or had to deal with political authority. While they largely reflect the changing historical conditions of early, middle, and late twentieth-century Arab socio-political and cultural conditions, the careers of these three figures also express, most deeply and extensively, themes that are common to generations of Arab intellectuals. In addition to the issue of coming to terms with the powers that be, these themes also include harmonizing local culture with western, and international, culture, the homeland and the attachment to place, and the issue of exile and identity.

The material here is more than can be covered in one chapter. Each of the three figures demands at least *one* separate chapter. The nature of the radicalism of each of the three figures may be distinguished as follows: Taha Hussain (1880–1973), a cultural rebel or radical, Al-Jawahiry (1899–1997), a social rebel and radical, and Edward Said (1935–2003), a nationalist radical.

Secondly, each of the three figures' intellectual development went into sharp opposition to authority. This opposition, however, was simultaneous with an imposed, inevitable, and unavoidable co-existence with authority. Having said that, distinctions or distinguishing features of time, place, and thrust of work of each of the three figures must be taken fully into account.

The question of identity is also very central to the discussion at hand, or the question of the global and the local in contemporary parlance. More specifically, one has to deal with the Europeanness of Taha Hussain, the Americanness of Edward Said, and the internationalness of Al-Jawahiry.

The initial uniqueness of each of the three figures is an amazing dimension that must be taken fully into account. The question of super-achievement, genius if you like, embodied in (a) the blindness of Taha Hussain, (b) the poetic gift of Al-Jawahiry, and (c) the scholarship of Edward Said, must not be lost sight of.

On the relationship with power, the path of all three figures inevitably involved compromises with dominant conservative culture (Taha Hussain), with dictatorship and the powers that be (Al-Jawahiry), and with the dominant powers (Edward Said).

The full analysis of these issues (identity, opposition, authority, achievement or genius) will, at some stage, require the deeper scrutiny of the three terms of the title of the paper: Radical, Arab, Intellectual.

This leads also to the wider issue of the role and place of the intellectual in society. We may remember here Sartre's remark about the (positive) death of the intellectual who is ideally to be replaced, or whose role is to be replaced, by that of the people. (In contrast, to the (negative) death of the intellectual, when he, like the people, is silenced).

Aside from the specific limitations and gaps in the thought of each of the three figures, one may keep in mind the ultimate limitation imposed by their social and historical conditions and related to the wider issues of internationalism and global cultural currents and transformations.

The specificity of the Arab situation, marked by despotism and near total absence of democracy necessitating those compromises, must be taken into account. The other specificity of the Arab situation that is consequent upon the extreme despotism, is the ultimate *weakness* of the despot when he faces the free, radical intellectual, who winning an easy victory through his outstanding intellectual achievements, *rises above the limits of the power of the despot* who can hardly touch him any longer.

One aspect of the internal contradiction in Said's thought, astutely identified by Aijaz Ahmad, involves the obvious disharmony between his Auerbachian humanism and his Foucaultian anti-humanism, Benda's anti-socialism and Gramsci's Marxism, as well as in his political positions (e.g. with Arafat and against Arafat, with peace with Israel and against peace with Israel, and so on). Similar contradictions can be detected in Taha Hussain and Al-Jawahiry—in being against tyrannical authority and compromising (necessarily) with it. Said's anti-Marxism (discussed in Ahmad, 1992, 177–9, 193, 195, 198–203, Sprinker, 1992, 94–5, 259–262, as well as his own *Orientalism*, 1978) should also be compared with Taha Hussain's position (an ally?) and Al-Jawahiry's (an advocate).

The question of identity (and the duality and, indeed, multi-facetedness of identity) is brought up at several crucial places in Said's autobiography *Out of Place* (2000). In the very opening pages, we come across statements like: "the travails of bearing such a name [i.e. the Arabic Said coupled with the English Edward] were compounded by an equally unsettling quandary when it came to language. I have never known what language I spoke first, Arabic or English, or which one was really mine beyond any doubt. What I do know, however, is that the two have always been together in my life, one resonating in the other, sometimes ironically, sometimes nostalgically, most often each correcting, and commenting on, the other. Each *can* seem like my absolutely first language, but neither is" (2000, 4). A little further on, Said adds, "I have retained this unsettled sense of many identities—mostly in conflict with each other—all my life, together with an acute memory of the despairing feeling that I wish we could have been all-Arab, or all-European or American, or all-Orthodox Christian, or all-Muslim, or all-Egyptian, and so on" (2000, 5). Even as a family in Cairo, in his early years, Said felt this phenomenon: "We were all Shawam, amphibious Levantine creatures whose essential lostness was momentarily stayed by a kind of forgetfulness, a kind of daydream, that included elaborate catered dresser parties, outings to fashionable restaurants, the opera, ballet, and concerts. By the end of the forties, we were no longer Shawam but *khawagat*, the designated and respectful title for foreigners which, as used by Muslim Egyptians, has always carried a tinge of hostility. Despite the fact that I spoke—and I thought looked—like a native Egyptian, something seemed to give me away. I resented the implication that I was somehow a foreigner, even though deep down I knew that to them I was, despite being an Arab" (2000, 195). Said further on does add that: "My growing sense of Palestinian identity (thanks to Aunt Nabila) refused the demeaning label, partly because my emerging consciousness of myself as something altogether more complex and authentic than a colonial mimic simply refused" (2000, 195). The new consciousness of identity was not to develop fully, however, until decades later: "I was no longer the same person after 1967; the shock of that war drove me back to where it had all started, the struggle over Palestine" (2000, 293).

What needs to be mentioned here is that this consciousness of identity accompanied Edward Said's general intellectual development, which may be described as having taken an upwardly moving trajectory course from the publication of his *Orientalism* in 1978 until his death in 2003. The best proof of that is his last book, *Humanism and Democratic Criticism*, published after his death in 2004, which contains a positive, intellectual refutation of Samuel Huntington, Fukuyama, Lyotard, and Harold Bloom. In addition, it also contains a new realization of the intellectual errors of his *Orientalism,* and an enjoyable commentary on the relationship between culture and civilization, on the one hand, and barbarism and decadence, on the other. This remains an accurate evaluation of the book, in spite of its tendency sometimes to oversimplify, as, for example, in his affirmation, in the very opening pages of the book that he is an American, that the United States is the world's only superpower, that he grew up in a non-western tradition, and that the events of September 11 have changed the US and the world as a whole, as if these four items were great truths and not just words, which may not, in fact, transmit any important concepts at all, a procedure, which indeed reminds us of the kind of erroneous and "orientalist" remarks found in his first published work, *Beginnings* (1975)[1]

A similar question of identity, though in somewhat of a reverse direction, will fruitfully be discussed in relation to how Taha Hussain's European (or better, Mediterranean) identity, as idea and as practice, grew out of his Arab-Islamic and specifically Egyptian identity (and indeed co-existed with it). In a previous study, I reached the conclusion that "it is perhaps Taha Hussain's radical, humanist secularism, more than anything else, that lies behind his "Mediterraneanism" and his call for the "Europeanization" of Egyptian culture. At its heart lies the key element of progressivism that charts for the Egyptian cultural project the almost inevitable "European", i.e. modern and scientific, road for advance, rejecting the cobwebs of reaction embedded in both the backward Islamist straitjacket and the chauvinistic, and often equally backward, Pan-Arabist rhetoric. In the field of literature, Taha Hussain's principal domain, he courageously and unflinchingly advocated the transfer of modern, western approaches to the study of literature in Egypt. For Taha Hussain, ancient Egyptian culture, the heritage of Arab/ Islamic culture, and, finally, modern "European" culture could and should co-exist harmoniously, in order to advance along the one and the same road of universal human progress" (Al-Dabbagh, 2006, 360–1).

Al-Jawahiry's internationalist identity, again both in theory and in practice, also grew out of his Arab-Islamic and uniquely Iraqi identity but also co-existed with it. Al-Jawahiry, like the whole Iraqi school of modern poetry, which included poets like Al-Sayyab, Al-Bayaty, and Al-Haydary, played a vital role in the formation and rejuvenation of Arabic poetry in the twentieth century. And, like the other poets of this Iraqi school, while formed by the experience of exile that helped to bring them closer to world literary heritage, remained intimately bound both to the rich, cultural heritage of his country and to the social and political circumstances that affected the lives of his people.

In a previous study, I have explained that while "the spaces of the Iraqi poets' exile extend from the neighbouring Arab countries (the Kuwait of Al-Sayyab, the Syria of Al-Jawahiry, the Cairo and Amman of Al-Bayaty, and so on) to European countries (the Prague of Al-Jawahiry, the Moscow and Madrid of Al-Bayaty, the London of Al-Haydary, and of others), the inner spaces from which the elements of the new poetics of exile and identity are formed, however, are no less important. These cover geography (Tigris and the Euphrates, palm tress, and other distinct Iraqi features), cultural history and Arab/Islamic heritage (the classical poets in the case of Al-Jawahiry and the heritage of Sufism in the case of Al-Bayaty stand out as two prominent examples), ancient mythology (particularly Mesopotamian mythology), modernity (largely through English literature, as in Al-Sayyab, Al-Bayaty, and Al-Haydary), and internationalism (largely through world literature, as in Al-Jawahiry and Al-Bayaty), giving rise to a distinctive poetic voice that can be characterized by the following features: It is a populist voice, in the sense that it is first and foremost the voice of the people of Iraq against their oppressors, in the various epochs and eras. At the same time, it is not a narrowly nationalist, and certainly not a chauvinist, or racist, voice. It is also definitely not fundamentalist; indeed, not even religious in the strict sense of the word, although it can be quite spiritual in the broadest way. It is a basically progressive and democratic voice that can be described as leftist, and indeed even Marxist at times, in its general tendency. It is a voice that represents the two major nations of Iraq, the Arabs and the Kurds, and successfully embodies the unifying elements of modern Iraqi culture as well as ancient Mesopotamian civilization. Above all, it is a radical and revolutionary voice, one that contains the vision of a new identity and a new, more just and more happy, society. Lastly, it is a voice that echoes the old cultural and mythological resources of Iraq and, at the same time, also blends very successfully into the rich heritage of the world at large" (Al-Dabbagh, 2005, 6–7).

On the complex and contradictory nature of Said's relationship with authority, one should consult Nubar Hovsepian's excellent article, "Connections with Palestine", printed in Michael Sprinker's *Edward Said: A Critical Reader* (1992), to trace the development of that relationship. Hovsepian explains that: "Despite Said's scathing critique of Zionism, *The Question of Palestine* could also be interpreted as "An Essay of Reconciliation." When he wrote the book in 1977, it would be safe to say that most Palestinians did not concede that Jews had legitimate historical claims to Palestine. He has said: "I don't deny their claims, but their claim always entails Palestinian dispossession." Said does not dispute the Zionist claim outright, but he wishes to remind Zionists that they are encumbered with Palestinians and Palestinian history, a fact entailed by what they have done and are doing to historical Palestine. In this context, Edward W. Said, then member of the PNC, recognized that the desired solution for the conflict must provide for the inclusion of both the Jews of Israel and the Palestinians" (1992, 11). In fact, Hovsepian continues, "Said's essay in reconciliation is viewed by some radical Palestinians as having gone too far. He is accused of frittering away Palestinian national rights by making "unwarranted concessions to Zionism." Accordingly, Said's key failure is in defining the conflict as one "between two peoples," instead of a class struggle against Zionism and Imperialism. Said's failings are a function of his "bourgeois humanistic approach," which makes him distrustful of the power of "armed struggle", hence, he is seen as favoring a political solution" (1992, 12). Indeed, Hovsepian continues, "over time, "armed struggle" had to give way to politics and diplomacy. Already, in the seventies President Sadat was suggesting that the Palestinians form a government in exile. Indeed, both Sadat and Arafat suggested that Edward Said could be a member of such a government" (1992, 13). Iqbal Ahmad, the Pakistani radical and Said's friend, also confirms that Said was one of the early supporters of peace with Israel, and if Yaser Arafat had responded to that suggestion that he carried to Beirut in the autumn of 1978 and once again in March, 1979, it would have been possible to "reach a sensible Palestinian-Israeli settlement" (*The Pen and the Sword: Dialogues with David Barsamian*, translated into Arabic by Tawfiq Al-Asadi, 2004) (Said, 2004, 11). The fact that Said later grew, after the Oslo agreements, to become the foremost critic of the Palestinian political authority does not delete his initial position, nor does it remove the key internal contradiction of being opposed to authority and representing it at the same time.

The dualistic and divided nature of Al-Jawahiry's attitude towards power and authority appear in the very early stages of his public life and continues, as a key feature, until his death. This can be seen from the early establishment of his special relationship with King Faisal I and later with the ruling Hashemite family, in the 1920s (Jalel Al-Attiya, *Al-Jawahiry: A Poet of the Twentieth Century*, 1998, 49–51, and Sulaiman Jabran, *The Combination of Opposites: A Study in the Life and Poetry of Al-Jawahiry*, 2003, 35–8, 56), which continued despite his growing rebelliousness and populism in his maintenance of a close relationship with King Ghazi, and later with Prince Abdul-Ilah and Nuri Al-Said, in the 30s and early 40s (Al-Attiya, 1998, 63–4, Jabran, 2003, 40), and down to his poem on the coronation of Faisal II in 1953 (Jabran, 2003, 56), and his poem celebrating King Hussain's 40th anniversary of his coronation in 1993, actually a re-doing of a poem written originally to Abdul-Ilah. Intermittent with this relationship was the same divided and dualistic nature of Al-Jawahiry's support, and later denunciation, of Bakr Sidqi's 1936 coup (Al-Attiya, 1998, 63–4), his special relationship, turned later into antagonism and confrontation, with Abdul-Karim Qasim (Al-Attiya, 1998, 69–76, Jabran, 2003, 59–60), and his complex relationship with the Baath regime in Iraq (Al-Attiya, 1998, 127–140).

In tracing the life and works of Al-Jawahiry, one may well detect echoes of the traditional role of the poet in classical Arab society and his reliance on patronage. Here it will be important to remember the specificity of the Arab nature of this relationship as well as the specific nature of Al-Jawahiry's embodiment of it—his embarrassment by it together with his continuation of it. (See, for this, Hasan Alawy's article, "Al-Jawahiry: Poems Born of the Civilization of Al-Kufa" in Khayal Muhammad Mahdi Al-Jawahiry, *Al-Jawahiry: The Symphony of Departure*, 1999, 99–116, especially 109–111). The co-existence of this dependency with his almost total rebelliousness and rejection of political authority is also a feature of Al-Jawahiry's career. (See Majeed Al-Radhy, "Al-Jawahiry between Opposition to Tyranny and Exile", in Khayal, 1999, 128–150, and Shawqi Baghdadi, "Al-Jawahiry as a Person and as

I Knew Him", Khayal, 1999, 157–163). It is also important to remember that in the later stages of his life, the poet may well have come to regard himself, like Al-Mutanabby, as rising way above the politicians he praised and, therefore, as untouched by any compromises such praise may have entailed. (See Abdul-Rahman Munif, "Al-Jawahiry's Journey and Departure: The Legend of a Century", Khayal, 1999, 226–232, especially 228–9).

Perhaps the best summing-up of Taha Hussain as the eternal transformer and compromiser is still Fathy Ghanim's 1954 article in *Akher Sa'aa*, quoted in Anwar Al-Jundy's *The Trial of Taha Hussain's Thought*, 1984, 87–93. Ghanim used the expression *Bayna Bayn* (i.e. uncommitted hedger and conciliator) to describe not only Taha Hussain's oscillations between faith and non-faith, liberalism and conservatism, *Wafd* and anti-*Wafd*, the Left and the Right, Royalism and Republicanism, but also his language and literary style, which was a combination of the old, classical, and new, modern styles, that was used to cover his oscillation between contradictory ideas and his refusal to commit to either side of the duality, almost as if he were saying, in a narcissistic mode reminiscent of Al-Jawahiry, that he, as Taha Hussain, was more important than these contradictions. Significantly, one of the best book-length studies of Taha Hussain is aptly named *The Transformations of Taha Hussain*, by Mustafa Abdul-Ghany, 1990.

In conclusion, it is important to be aware of the evolution of the thought and outlook of each of these three figures. This awareness is crucial for understanding not only the development of their identity (or identities) referred to earlier, but also their *intellectual* development. Interestingly, all three died at the summit of their achievement. This is especially true of Edward Said, who died at the age of sixty-eight. Taha Hussain and Al-Jawahiry had already reached a height from which they did not decline or relapse. Although compromises with authority and the internal contradictions mentioned earlier continued, perhaps indicating a permanent feature of their careers and situation imposed by the times, all three departed on a radical and rebellious note that best sums up their lives and works.

· 9 ·

MEDITERRANEANISM IN MODERN ARAB CULTURAL THOUGHT

In the opening "ideological" chapters of his *The Future of Culture in Egypt* (1938),[1] Taha Hussain (1889–1973) raises the question whether Egypt belongs culturally to the East or to the West—with the clear implication that there are two distinct and separable Eastern and Western cultures. To clarify the question further he puts it in clear-cut terms: "Is the Egyptian mind Eastern in its imagination, comprehension, and judgment of things or is it Western? In other words, is it easier for the Egyptian mind to understand a Chinaman or a Japanese person, or is it easier for it to understand a Frenchman or an Englishman?"[2]

Old-fashioned and blatantly politically incorrect as Taha Hussain's terms may seem, representing almost a perfect case, in fact, of oriental "orientalism", following up the elaboration of the answers to these introductory questions may well prove worth the effort.

Having dismissed the ancient cultures of the Far East as cultures that have no relevance to Egyptian culture, Taha Hussain moves to the far more controversial postulate of denying even its connection with the cultures of the Near East. "It is very clear," he claims, "that the Egyptian mind had no significant contact with the mind of the Far East, and lived a life, not of peace and cooperation, but of war and conflict, with the Persian mind."[3]

By contrast, Taha Hussain claims that the relationship between Egyptian and ancient Aegean cultures, between Egypt and the early epochs of Greek civilization, indeed between Egypt and Greece, from the sixth century B.C. to the days of Alexander, is indisputable. The inevitable conclusion is that "The Egyptian mind in its very early formation was a mind that, if affected by anything, was affected by the Mediterranean, and if it had mutual interests with anyone, it was with the peoples of the Mediterranean."[4]

Furthermore, it is not only Egyptian culture that has affected and was in turn affected by Greek culture, but also other Asian cultures of the region, such as that of the Chaldeans. On the basis of this "Greek connection", Taha Hussain moves, by way of marginalizing the role of both Christianity and Islam, to his major conclusion regarding the future of culture in Egypt. His argument is that just as "Christianity did not degrade the European mind and did not reverse its Greek heritage or its Mediterranean features, it must also be true that Islam did not change the Egyptian mind or the minds of the peoples of the Mediterranean that had adopted Islam."[5]

Consequently, the key question that raises itself for Taha Hussain is this: "Why does this sea [the Mediterranean] that gives rise to such an excellent and superior mind in the West, leave the East mindless, or gives it only a weak and decadent mind?" And the answer is that such a state of affairs should not blind us to the fact that "Egypt was always a part of Europe in everything that concerns intellectual and cultural life", or that there are any intellectual or cultural differences between the Mediterranean peoples,"[6] but that it is political and economic circumstances that favour certain of these peoples at certain times and others at other times. And the key lesson for the future of the Egyptians culturally is to Europeanize.

The course of the argument which, as has been shown, sounds quaintly "orientalist" to our post-Saidian ears leads in the end to daringly pioneering conclusions that remain relevant and challenging even today—to the questions of cultural identity as well as those of East/West relations.

Taha Hussain's call for what might be termed wholesale Europeanization— "We have to become Europeans in everything, accepting both good and bad . . . We have to walk their way and follow their path in order to be equals to them and partners with them in civilization, in both its good aspects and its bad aspects, its sweetness and its bitterness, what is liked and what is disliked, what is praised and what is shameful"[7]—stems, in fact, from his rejection of the old "orientalist" distinction between the materialism of the West and the spirituality of the East, as well his dismissal of the conventional xenophobic charge that modern civilization is a threat to national identity. "I do not know why Egyptian national identity will be lost if they followed the Europeans any more than the Japanese have lost their identity, when Egypt has as glorious a culture as Japan?"[8] he asks pointedly.

Arguing against the so-called spirituality of the East, which he sees as largely associated with the Far, rather than the Near, East, Taha Hussain asks his compatriots: do we want to adopt Far Eastern religion and philosophy or do we want to follow the way they are accepting and following the path of modern European civilization, in industry, in education, and in the political system, as Japan and China have done or are doing?[9] His conclusion, indeed, is refreshingly contemporary and universalist and the very opposite of "orientalist" modes of thinking:

"These countries that lie on the shore of the Mediterranean and that extend from Iraq to Syria and Lebanon and to Palestine and Egypt, do not differ in their civilization from European civilization because both civilizations are the summation or the result of ancient civilizations that reached Europe through Greece. The future of civilization in the East and in the West and its future in Europe is one and can only be one. And after all, how can we in the Near East form independent peoples and sovereign nations that can reach the level of European civilization if we do not adopt the basic material principles of this civilization?"[10]

In almost identical terms, Salama Mousa (1887–1958), in several articles published between 1927 and 1930, had, in fact, preceded Taha Hussain in arguing that contrary to the current inclination among Egyptians to sympathize with Asia and with the culture of the East and to regard Europeans with fear and suspicion, as in the Russo-Japanese war, when most people supported the Japanese and were happy that Russia was defeated and seemed to agree with their depiction by the newspapers as an oriental nation like the Japanese, Egyptians, in fact, had much more in common with Europeans than with the peoples of the Far East, and were indeed much closer to the Russians, in terms of culture and religion, as well as race, than they are to the Japanese.

Using social-Darwinist and racial terminology that seems to have been still current at the time, and not as politically incorrect as they are nowadays, Salama Mousa argues that "The brown peoples all belong to European races that inhabited Europe before being occupied by the Asians, and that the skulls of the ancient Egyptians are identical to those discovered currently in England and which belonged to the inhabitants of the British Isles three thousand years ago."[11] Covered by the Roman Empire, monotheism and Greek thought, the Egyptians as well as the Syrians and all the inhabitants of the Arab world from Baghdad to Tangier, had the same western heritage. To sum it up, Salama Mousa says, "We are Europeans in blood, personal inclination, culture, and language. Therefore, it is not correct to say that we are orientals unless it is meant to say that we are part of the Eastern Roman Empire, which is not I think what is meant usually by our orientalism."[12] And even though, he continues, "Turks and Tatars ruled us for a thousand years and corrupted our civilization to the extent that this corruption went into our blood, we still remain, in make-up and inclination, European."[13] Salama Mousa's conclusion is the same as Taha Hussain's:

"I see that it is in our interest and in the interest of the whole world which in fact should be more important and more crucial than our own interest, that we plant it in the minds of all the Arabs in Egypt, Iraq, Syria, and North Africa that they are Europeans in race, culture, and civilization and that they should accompany the most advanced European nations in culture and customs. This was the aim of Ismail Pasha, the Khedive of Egypt, who is truly the father of the modern Egyptian renaissance, and who tried to make Egypt a part of Europe and made us dress as they did, eat as they did, and in fact, went as far as giving our notables fair-skinned women so that our brownness disappears and we begin to resemble the Europeans in everything."[14]

Salama Mousa elaborated his argument in a lengthier essay, entitled "Hesitation between East and West" which was published in the following year[15] reiterating the same points and adding others regarding use of the vernacular, the revival of ancient Egyptian culture and the rejection of any form of oriental league or religious league. His call for Europeanization now even extends, à la Attaturk, to the wearing of the western hat, "as a symbol of civilization." More significantly, Salama Mousa's second essay reveals an *avant la lettre* awareness of globalism and of the necessity for Egypt to be part of the global community. "Our patriotism should be loyal and enlightened. If we are willing to sacrifice ourselves for Egypt, then we should be willing to sacrifice Egypt for the world. The world is our bigger homeland. Our patriotism does not lie in that we love Egypt more than the world, but that we can serve her more than we can serve the world, because we know her and know her weaknesses and deficiencies better. We can serve the world less because we know less about it."[16]

In 1930, the University of Egypt organized a debate on Kipling's famous dictum, "East is East and West is West and ne'er the Twain shall Meet" which was supported by Al-Akkad (who won with 228 votes) and opposed by Salama

Mousa (who lost with 132 votes). Significantly, Al-Akkad's defense is lost, but Salama Mousa's speech is available and has bee reprinted.[17] It is interesting that Salama Mousa, who calls for the abolition of East/West distinctions and argues indeed for their non-existence as far as Egypt and the Near East are concerned, forming as they do essentially the same civilization as Europe, finds that his position works ultimately for the cause of universal brotherhood and humanism, while the insistence on insurmountable East/West distinctions serves as a justification for colonialism and imperialism for which Kipling, for this reason, is the unrivalled poet.

The issue of East/West cultural relations and East/West cultural identity was central to the Egyptian intellectual scene, and other Egyptian intellectuals, particularly the novelist Tawfiq Al-Hakim,[18] were preoccupied with it. Tawfiq al-Hakim expressed his open admiration for the West, and called for its emulation by the Egyptians. In articles published in the thirties and forties, he argued that Eastern culture must catch up with Western culture and assimilate it as its own. He laments the fact that, in the heyday of Islamic civilization, only the works of Greek philosophy and science were translated into Arabic, and not the literary products of Greco-Roman culture, and he warns Egyptians not to repeat the same mistake, but to learn and borrow from all aspects of Western culture. Again, in what nowadays would be regarded as oddly "orientalist", Hakim, like Taha Hussain and Salama Mousa, paints a stark contrast between the "lethargic East" and the "vibrant West" to underline his call for modernization in all aspects of life, ranging from cultural issues to the position of women in society, and the call for democracy, self-reliance and the individualistic spirit, a project which he, himself, as a writer, put into practice by pioneering the introduction into Arabic literature of the western genres of drama and the novel.

Old-fashioned, "orientalist", and glaringly politically incorrect, as the terms and formulations of Taha Hussain, Salama Mousa, and Tawfiq Al-Hakim may seem today, the arguments that they developed and the conclusions that they reached have aroused interest and controversy from the start and may well prove relevant even now. Vehemently, but also one-sidedly and irrationally, rejected in the height of Pan-Arabism, in the sixties extending into seventies,[19] and of Islamism, in the eighties extending into the nineties,[20] perhaps it is only now in the twenty-first century that a balanced and objective evaluation of these two writers' important contribution to cultural ideology and cultural identity may be achieved, even though some of the most astute contemporary commentators continue to have reservations about their works.[21]

All three writers, Salama Mousa, Tawfiq Al-Hakim, and Taha Hussain, particularly Taha Hussain, were involved in controversies and debates on a variety of literary, cultural, and political issues. On the topic addressed by this paper, the vantage point of the three writers was quite similar and often faced an opposition to which they felt that they had to respond. Thus Salama Mousa, for example, defended his cultural views by explaining that they called for the study of Pharaonic Egypt not because they were reactionaries, but because, as Egyptians, they owed a natural allegiance to the Nile Valley in which they had lived for thousands of years. He regarded as absurd the claims that they would thus become anti-Arab, or that they would call for a revival of ancient Egyptian religions and customs. Nor were they against the unity of the Arabs. They had a right simply to be proud of an ancient civilization of which the whole world was, indeed, rightly proud.[22]

Similarly, Taha Hussain felt that he had to defend his call for the protection of ancient Egyptian heritage against the attacks of the Pan-Arabists: "Egypt is rightly proud and protective of its Pharaonic history and heritage. It would, however, be an absurdity to misinterpret this as a call for a return to Pharaonic religion, or for the replacement of Arabic by ancient Egyptian, or the replacement of the modern democratic system by the ancient Pharaonic system."[23] Tawfiq Al-Hakim, too, joined his two colleagues in defending the call for a kind of wholesale westernization, declaring: "If we are unable to create an Eastern civilization, let us do what Turkey did and simply join the group of the European nations."[24]

Of all the charges, ranging from anti-Islamism to Zionism to surrender to European Imperialism, that Taha Hussain and Salama Mousa have been accused of, a sympathy for the Left, crudely reduced to "Communism", is perhaps the only one that may have a substance of truth in it. Salama Mousa, of course, was one of the founders of the Egyptian Socialist Party in 1921, with whom Taha Hussain retained a special relationship, intellectually as well as personally, throughout his life. In fact, recent studies have confirmed both Salama Mousa's strong admiration (to the point of allegiance) for Marxism, and his widespread influence on a whole generation of pioneering Egyptian intellectuals that includes such figures as Taha Hussain, Tawfiq Al-Hakim, and Najeeb Mahfouz.[25]

Accusations of "Leftism" and "Communism" were, perhaps, first hurled at Taha Hussain, however, after the publication of his short stories in 1946, which were later collected in one volume under the title of *Al-Mu'aththaboona fil Ardh* (The wretched of the Earth). These stories were an explicit condemnation of the feudal system in the Egyptian countryside, as reflected in the life of the peasantry and the oppression of the landlords.

Taha Hussain's "Marxist" leanings, however, could perhaps be also deduced from his critical methodology, particularly his focus on the socio-economic relations that underlie historical events, his objectivity and his rejection of received notions, as well as his sensitive and sympathetic attention to such figures as Ibn Khaldun, and such socio-political movements as the "communistic" *Thawrat Al-Zunj* (The Revolt of the Slaves) in Islamic history.

In the modern times, when Taha Hussain was accused on the pages of *Al-Fajr Al-Jadeed* (The New Dawn), a left-wing Egyptian magazine of the forties, of being a bourgeois writer, he felt obliged to write to it, in his own defense, that he resented being called a bourgeois writer, and that he was a populist, or a man of the people, in upbringing as well as education, and that he never thought literature could be isolated from the people, but that, in fact, all high literature could only retain its position if it addressed the people and the people alone. To the same magazine, he wrote in 1945, "if I have to reveal my social and political beliefs, then let it be known that I do not like conservative, or even moderate, democracy, nor am I satisfied with a lukewarm socialism, but I like to go to the extreme left as much as I can."[26] Finally, Taha Hussain's contemporary detractors have not failed to hurl the charge of "Communism", among other things, at him for his acknowledged influence on such "Marxist" writers as Abdul-Adheem Anees, Kamil Zuhry, Abdul-Rahman Al-Sharqawi, and Mohammad Mandur, and his defense and help of some of them, like Abdul-Adheem Anees, when they were arrested or dismissed from their jobs.

In summing up, it is perhaps Taha Hussain's radical, humanist secularism, more than anything else, that lies behind his "Mediterraneanism" and his call for the "Europeanization" of Egyptian culture. At its heart lies the key element of progressivism that charts for the Egyptian cultural project the almost inevitable "European", i.e. modern and scientific, road for advance, rejecting the cobwebs of reaction embedded in both the backward Islamist straitjacket and the chauvinistic, and often equally backward, Pan-Arabist rhetoric. In the field of literature, Taha Hussain's principal domain, he courageously and unflinchingly advocated the transfer of modern, western approaches to the study of literature in Egypt. For Taha Hussain, ancient Egyptian culture, the heritage of Arab/Islamic culture, and, finally, modern "European" culture, could and should co-exist harmoniously, in order to advance along the one and the same road of universal human progress. It would not be anachronistic, I think, to describe Taha Hussain, of the early decades of the twentieth-century, as a contemporary secular universalist of the first years of the twenty-first.

The continuing strength of this radical, secularist tradition of Salama Mousa, Taha Hussain, and Tawfiq Al-Hakim is confirmed by its widespread influence, not only in Egypt, but in the Arab world as a whole. Recent studies have, in fact, deepened our understanding of the scope as well as the militancy of this pioneering, cultural movement.[27] If one were to single out one figure, however, to demonstrate the strength of this influence in the literary and cultural field, particularly with regard to the Mediterranean concerns of this paper, the choice might well fall on the Egyptian writer and critic, Lewis Awadh (1915–1990), as the best representative of the second generation that carried further the work of those pioneers.

In a series of articles, spanning nearly two decades,[28] Lewis Awadh addressed, in a more academic and scholarly fashion perhaps, the "Mediterranean idea" that first appeared so casually and spontaneously in those early essays of Taha Hussain and Salama Mousa. In the first of these articles, originally delivered as a paper entitled, "The Distinguishing Features of Mediterranean Culture", in a conference on Mediterraneanism held in Florence in 1972, Lewis Awadh focuses in much greater detail than his two illustrious predecessors on the common ontological and mythological basis of the original religious beliefs of the region. Through this entry into the subject, the unity of the variety of Egyptian, Greek, and Mesopotamian elements becomes much clearer. Thus, for example, Lewis Awadh concludes, "It is clear that all the religions of the great Mediterranean basin, whether pagan or monotheistic, share one metaphysical and symbolic structure, that revolves around the idea of salvation, or renewal, or sacrifice through the suffering of a God, a demi-god, a Titan, or a tortured hero."[29]

Furthermore, Lewis Awadh argues that, in addition to this metaphysical/symbolic structure that is the unique contribution of Mediterranean culture, the ability to unite subjectivity with the objective depiction of God or of the World is also one of the distinguishing features of Mediterranean culture. The outer world can only be understood through the inner world of mind, sense, subjectivity, intuition, and so on. Hence the necessity of theory. And the search for theory has been the common pursuit, according to Lewis Awadh, of all prophets, philosophers, Sufis, Saints, and heretics produced at the shores of the Mediterranean.

While there is undoubtedly a degree of this dualism in all cultures of the world, it is more dominant in some than in others. In Anglo-Saxon culture, for example, Lewis Awadh contends, the movement is not from the macrocosm to the microcosm, but vice versa. Therefore, such a culture leans more to the deductive rather than the inductive method, and tends to be more empirical than abstract, more pragmatic and relative than clear-cut and absolute, more flexible than committed.[30]

Lewis Awadh also does not rest with these basic distinctions, but goes on to elaborate that one should also recognize the diversity of Mediterranean religions and philosophies in spite of their unity of metaphysics and symbolic structure. And while the common denominator may be this deep sense of the duality of life, of mind and matter, thought and existence, good and evil, there are widely diverging expressions of this human predicament and dilemma in the religions and cultures of the Mediterranean.

Lewis Awadh goes back to this theme in another paper entitled, "The Struggle of Opposites", published in 1977, (99–104), and, six years later, in 1983, in a paper delivered at a conference in Marseilles entitled, "Egypt Faces its Past" (125–134), applies these ideas to the history and contradictions of Egyptian cultural identity, paying due homage to the pioneering ideas of Taha Hussain and Tawfiq Al-Hakim in underlining the Mediterranean nature of Egyptian culture that complements its Arab/Islamic features. And in yet another article published in the same year under the title of "The Story of Secularism in Egypt" (135–148), Lewis Awadh places the Mediterranean cultural perspective of the pioneers, and the modernizing, secularizing, and Europeanizing project that it entailed, within the socio-historical context of the development of secularism in Egypt, from the Napoleonic Campaign of 1798, through the modernization experiment of Mohammad Ali (1805–1840), through the liberal democratic period of 1919–1952, and down, finally, to the "revolutionary" and "post-revolutionary" periods of Nasser and beyond. It is indicative yet again of the continuing relevance and strength of this tradition that Lewis Awadh, in a paper entitled "East Faces West" (217–230), originally a lecture delivered at a conference in Rome in 1975, is able to place these earlier concerns about East/West relations and Egyptian cultural identity within the new world-historical perspective of the nineteen seventies, thus summing up the achievement of those pioneering figures, but also brilliantly foreshadowing the concepts of orientalism, humanism, and universalism that were to dominate literary and cultural discussion in the last two decades of the twentieth century. And although this last paper, written in the epoch of the Vietnam war, traces the history of the confrontation between East and West from the Greek-Persian wars, to the Roman Empire, the rise of Islam, the Crusades, and the Islamic empires of the 16th century, down to modern European colonialism and contemporary western imperialism, it continues implicitly to pay homage to those radical, secularist writers, by affirming the underlying unity of human civilization (in spite of the political and military East/West clashes), and rejecting all approaches that postulate a fundamental or inborn cultural confrontation between East and West.

· 1 0 ·

POETICS OF EXILE AND IDENTITY: THE CASE OF MODERN IRAQI POETRY

On the question of exile, contrasting, and even conflicting, estimates have tended to exist side by side. Exile has been regarded in the same breath as both a universal human condition and as a unique state of suffering and hardship that befalls certain unfortunate individuals and groups. Similarly, while the condition of exile and un-belonging to a native place, or indeed to any place, has been celebrated by some postcolonial writers and critics, the traditional view of exile, from Socrates and Ovid down to the varieties of political exile in modern times, has usually been negative. And while, at certain times and in certain cases, writers and intellectuals have voluntarily chosen exile, as in the two famous examples of the "lost generation" of American writers in the early twentieth century and the postcolonial writers and critics of our era, and have defended, indeed enjoyed and celebrated, their condition of *self*-exile, the majority of modern writers and intellectuals have tended to be forced under circumstances of political oppression to go into exile against their will.

In parallel with this process, writers and intellectuals have been able to create a poetics of exile through which they have been able to overthrow the condition of exile and the state of unbelonging *imaginatively* and, indeed, to transform them into a positive force through which the experience of alienation produced by exile becomes one of belonging to a wider community. This is the great achievement of exiled poets and writers from Dante down to our modern times. Feeling at home, so to speak, in the universe as a whole, after having been exiled from one's native town, or country, is an experience that extends from the Sufis, saints, and travelers of the medieval times to the multicultural writers of our own globalist era. Thus the experience of exile, painful as it no doubt is, has been able to serve as a magically imaginative adventure for the poet. The journey that it entails, of new spaces, new discoveries and new perspectives, is precisely what the poet needs as trigger for his creativity. Exile becomes the perfect setting for the defamiliarization necessary to initiate the artistic process.

Certain trends in postcolonial discourse, however, that derive ultimately from Edward Said's *Culture and Imperialism* (1993), in jubilation over the liberating experience of unbelonging that seems to come with exile, have wanted to dispense altogether with the whole idea of a national identity and a national culture. Based on the wrong assumption, perhaps embedded in the very term postcolonial, that we live in an era in which colonialism (and by implication also imperialism) have ceased to exist, the central argument of these writers has been that we should also do away with all nations and national identities as parts of a polarity that is no longer meaningful. In an oddly misconstrued and utopian conception, all frontiers are said to have disappeared and all nations, because they are hybrid and heterogeneous, are deemed to be non-existent.

Uniquely, both in the regional and the global contexts, modern Iraqi poetry was formed through the experience of exile and through the varieties of movement in space that it entailed. The major poets of the twentieth-century, Al-Jawahiry, Al-Bayaty, Buland Al-Haydary and Al-Sayyab, who played such a crucial role in the formation of modern Iraqi poetry, as well as Arabic poetry generally, all lived for long periods of their lives outside their country, and all, in fact, died in exile.

In stark contrast to the postmodernist and postcolonialist celebration and glorification of "hybridity" and "loss of identity", which in effect serves ultimately only to bolster the lines of demarcation, guarding both literary being and literary expression, established by the powers that dominate the world system, modern Iraqi poets who played a vital role in the formation and rejuvenation of Arabic poetry in the twentieth century, while formed by the experience of exile that helped to bring them closer to world literary heritage, remained intimately bound both to the rich cultural heritage and to the contemporary social circumstances that affected the lives of the Iraqis. Far from wanting to escape a national identity into a vague "in-between" state of "un-belonging", these poets were, in fact, instrumental in the very formation of a modern Iraqi identity; an identity, furthermore, that far from the usual connotations of narrowness or xenophobia it may sometimes acquire, was truly cosmopolitan and open to the rich heritage both of world culture and of international literary practice.

The spaces of the Iraqi poets' exile extend from the neighbouring Arab countries (The Kuwait of Al-Sayyab, the Syria of Al-Jawahiry, the Cairo and Amman of Al-Bayaty, and so on) to European countries (the Prague of Al-Jawahiry, the Moscow and Madrid of Al-Bayaty, the London of Al-Haydary, and recently of Saady Yousef and others). The inner spaces, from which the elements of the new poetics of exile and identity are formed, however, are no less significant. These cover geography (Tigris and the Euphrates, palm trees, and other distinctly Iraqi features), cultural history and Arab/Islamic heritage (the classical poets in the case of Al-Jawahiry and the heritage of Sufism in the case of Al-Bayaty stand out as two prominent examples), ancient mythology (particularly Mesopotamian mythology), modernity (largely through English literature, as in Al-Sayyab, Al-Bayaty and Al-Haydary), and internationalism (largely through world literature, as in Al-Jawahiry and Al-Bayaty), giving rise to a new and distinctive poetic voice that can be characterized by the following features:

It is a populist voice, in the sense that it is first and foremost the voice of the people of Iraq against their oppressors, in the various epochs and eras. At the same time, it is not a narrowly nationalist, and certainly not a chauvinist or racist, voice. It is also definitely not fundamentalist; indeed, not even religious in a strict sense of the word, although it can be quite spiritual in the broadest way. It is a basically progressive and democratic voice that can be described as leftist, and indeed even Marxist at times, in its general tendency. It is a voice that represents the two major nations of Iraq, the Arabs and the Kurds, and successfully embodies the unifying elements in modern Iraqi culture as well as ancient Mesopotamian civilization. Above all, it is a radical and a revolutionary voice, one that contains the vision of a new identity and a new, more just and happier, society. Lastly, it is a voice that echoes the old cultural and mythological resources of Iraq and, at the same time, also blends very successfully into the rich heritage of the world at large.

In addition, however, this Iraqi expression of poetic exile, particularly in its second phase, covering the eighties and the nineties, acquires a very bitter satirical tone and a very deep sense of the complexities of human alienation in the so-called postmodernist, globalist, era. While a romantic, almost sentimental, yearning for the homeland, often metaphorically depicted as the beloved, dominated a strain in the poetry of the first phase, covering especially

the fifties, sixties and seventies, an equally strong sense of an internal alienation dominated the second phase, as the realization dawned upon the poets
that there would be no return to the homeland, and that going forward and
coming to terms with the conditions of exile and inner alienation were the
only options.

Al-Sayyab's lines from his well-known poem, "A Stranger on the Gulf",
probably epitomizes this romanticism of the first phase:

> I loved in you the Iraq of my soul,
> And I was inspired by you in it.
>   . . .
> If you came to me in the strange land, it would be no meeting,
> Only meeting you in Iraq would be a meeting.
> My blood yearns for you, as if my blood is all my desire,
> Hungers for you, like the hunger of the drowned for air,
> Like the yearning of the foetus to be born.
> I am amazed how traitors can betray,
> If one betrays what it means to be, then how can he be?
>   . . . .
> The sun is more beautiful in my country than elsewhere, and the darkness—even the
> darkness—there is more beautiful, because it embraces Iraq.

This romantic celebration of the homeland achieves its greatest expression, perhaps, in Al-Sayyab's famous Unshudat Al Matar (Rainsong) which,
although not written in a condition of exile, reaches that supreme artistic state
of becoming universally applicable to all conditions:

> Your eyes are two forests of palm trees at the hour of dawn
> Or two balconies gradually distanced from the moon.
> Your eyes when they smile make the grapes ripen
> And the lights dance . . . like the moons in a river
> Disturbed by the oars, and here at the hour of dawn,
> As if the stars have come alive in their depths.

These eyes that seem to be those of the beloved turn out to be, of course,
those of the homeland:

> And they sweat in a fog of creeping sadness,
> Like the sea held in the palms of the evening,
> The warmth of winter and the shiver of autumn,
> And death and birth, and darkness, and light,
> There wakes, filling my soul, the shiver of weeping,
> And a savage ecstasy embracing the sky

Like the ecstasy of the child fearful of the moon!
As if the rainbows are drinking the clouds
And drop by drop melting in the rain . . .
Drowning the laughter of the children in the vineyard,
And playing with the silence of the sparrows on the trees
Rainsong . . .
Rain . . .
Rain . . .
Rain . . .
The evening yawned, and the clouds are still there,
Sweeping what it can sweep of its heavy tears,
Like a child who has started to blabber before falling asleep:
His mother—whom he did not find when he woke up,
A year ago, and when he insisted on asking,
They said to him "She will return the day after tomorrow . . ."—
She must come back
Even though the comrades whispered that she is there
By the hillside sleeping the sleep of death
Eating of its soil and drinking of its rain
Like a sad fisherman collecting his net
And cursing the waters and fate
And spreading song when the moon is down.
Rain . . .
Rain . . .
Do you know what sadness is sent by the rain?
And how the drain pipes weep when it pours?
And how the lonely feels lost in it?
Endlessly—like spilt blood, like the hungry,
Like love, like children, like the dead—this is rain!
And your eyes take me round with the rain,
And across the waves of the Gulf lightening sweeps
The banks of Iraq with stars and shells,
As if wanting to rise,
But the night keeps covering it under a blanket of blood.
I cry to the Gulf: "O Gulf
O provider of pearls, and shells, and death!"
And the echo comes back
Like the a weeping song:
"O Gulf
"O provider of shells and death . . ."

I seem to hear Iraq hording thunder and lightening
In the plains and in the mountains
So that when it is over
The winds leave no trace of the old city in the valley.

I seem to hear the palm trees drinking rain,
And the villages crying in pain, and the migrants
Struggling with oars and axes
Against the storms of the Gulf, and the lightening, singing:
"Rain . . .
"Rain . . .
"Rain . . ."
And in Iraq there is hunger
And in Iraq there is plenty in harvest time
To feed the crows and the grasshoppers
And the mills turn
In the fields, surrounded by men
Rain . . .
Rain . . .
Rain . . .
How we wept the night we left
Till we got ill by the rain
Rain . . .
Rain . . .
And ever since we were small
The sky used to darken in winter
And rain poured
And every year—when earth got covered with grass—we got hungry
Not a year passed when Iraq did not go hungry
Rain . . .
Rain . . .
Rain . . .
In every drop of rain
Red or yellow from the paradise of flowers
In every tear of the hungry and the naked
In every drop of blood spilled from the slaves
There is a smile awaiting a new dawn
And a dimple brightening the face of the newly born
In the young world of tomorrow, the giver of life!
Rain . . .
Rain . . .
Rain . . .
Iraq will be green with Rain . . ."

The move from this essentially romantic expression to a more modern one appears first, perhaps, in the many poems and anthologies of Al-Bayaty, who spent a much longer stretch of his life (from the fifties, in fact, through the nineties, to his death in 1999) far from the Kuwait of Al-Sayyab's short exile (and life) in several Arab and European countries:

We die in our exiled alienation
But we are born anew
We love anew
Refuse anew
Rebel anew.

This voice is heard across four decades, as in the 1960 poem, "Why Are We in Exile?", subtitled, "The Refugees Ask:"

Why are we in silence
Dying?
And I had a house,
My own house,
And there you are
Without a heart
Without a voice
Crying, and saying
Why are we in exile
Dying?
Dying in silence.
Why don't we cry?
Over fire
Over thorn
We walked,
And my people walked,
Why are we, My God,
Without a homeland, without love,
Dying?
Dying in fear.
Why are we in exile,
Why are we, My God?

And in this short poem, one of his last, written shortly before his death in the late nineties:

Who owns the homeland?
Is it the hired gun and the jailer, my lady,
Or is it the rainmaker?
Nazik, Al-Sayyab and Al-Jawahiry?
Or those who steal the bread, the medicine,
And the homeland?

The same two phases appear clearly in the poetry of Buland Al-Haydary. The first is represented by his anthology, "Steps in Exile", published in Beirut in 1956, in protest against the "homeland" that had driven him to hopeless escape and exile, and the second is represented by his last anthology, "The Doors of the Narrow House", published in London in 1990, in which he says:

The border guards of the homeland—so hated
Have stripped me even of my skin and blood,
Even of the dream of being born again in my wound.
          . . .
They have cut off all my ten fingers,
And as a precaution,
They have cut off all my ten toes too.

Buland's poem, "Shall I Go Back—But to Who?" is, perhaps, the most representative of the second phase:

How overwhelming is the humiliation
Of exiled alienation.
How sad it is not to know yourself as a human being
Except in alienation.

Buland, however, like many of the Iraqi poets of exile, never wallowed in his despair, but kept on dreaming, however seemingly hopelessly, of a new and brighter dawn:

Baghdad
Who says that the dead are not alive
In the memory of the young, in the memory of the grandchildren?
Who says that those who died for you are dead?
They will come back tomorrow,
And in them we shall recognize the candles of our joys.

Al-Jawahiry, too, who represents a more classical embodiment of the poet of rebellion and militant political exile, is reconciled, towards the end, to the permanence of his condition, although again expressed in his typical mode of revolutionary optimism:

I am Iraq
My tongue is its heart,
My blood its Euphrates,
And my being its splintered parts.

And in a more nostalgic mood, he writes in one of his loveliest and best known poems of exile, "O Tigris of Plenty:"

I greet you from afar, so greet me back,
O Tigris of plenty,
O mother of gardens,
I greet you in thirst,
And in refuge, like that of
The pigeon hovering between land and water,
O Tigris of plenty,
O fountain that I am forced
Against my will
To leave from time to time.

Saady Yousef, representing the next generation, is also an Iraqi poet of exile. In his "A Personal Song", he says:

Blessed is the one who said
I know the road which leads to it;
Blessed is the one whose lips uttered the four
letters:
"Iraq, Iraq, nothing but Iraq."*
Distant missiles will applaud;
Soldiers armed to the teeth will storm us;
Minarets and houses will crumble;
Palm trees will collapse under the bombing;
The shores will be crowded
With floating corpses.
We will seldom see Al-Tahrir Square
In books of elegies and photographs;
Restaurants and hotels will be our roadmaps
And our home in the paradise of shelter:
MacDonalds'
KFC
Holiday Inn;
And we will be drowned
Like your name, O Iraq,
"Iraq, Iraq, nothing but Iraq"

London, March 15, 2003

From the same generation, Muthaffar Al-Nawwab, in a poem titled "Wine and Grief", says:

The tavern is asleep.
Forgive me, I will leave now.
My heart is filled with wine and grief:
I wish I could roll in the sand

And the scent of melon
On the banks of the Tigris.

. . .

I hear an infant crying in his cradle:
Please God, let him have a homeland
I lived without one!

. . .

Baghdad wakes up from her dream,
Naked;
She washes her beauty with dew
And twilight blueness;
She goes inside to God
And comes out carrying the Sun
And some mint tea from Basra.
The banks of the Tigris are still asleep:
The informant forgot his report
On the table and is gone.
The report says: the wine is bad.
He lies about everything,
Even about the wine!

The continuation of this theme in the poetry of the latest generation
(the post-Saady and Nawwab generation) of Iraqi poets is, perhaps, best represented in this poem by Muayyad Al-Shaibany, titled appropriately enough,
"Abdul-Wahab Al-Bayaty:"

Now, Sir,
I see you in Amman
I see you in Madrid
I see you in Rasheed Street
And I see you in Shiraz
    In Damascus
    And in Al-Hussain Mosque
Swearing, mocking, or getting drunk,
    Or being spilled
    Like the blood of Iraq.
I see you in the café, but without a newspaper.
What is the need of a poet for a newspaper,
When he knows what happens in faraway times?
O, master of the first amplitude,
O, master of the poem,
O, fearless dead one,
Alone in exile fighting depression,
Resting, tired, over the blood of writing.

I see you in your faraway house,
I see you in your loneliness,
Dispersing the evening, the smoke, and the loved ones,
Suspending time on the doors,
And sitting upon the couch of doom
To start the journey once again . . .

Towards the end of an eloquent article, called "Reflections on Exile", which also gives its title to his latest collection of essays, Edward Said, whose work, more than that of any other contemporary literary and cultural critic, has been responsible for establishing the climate and the terms of our approach to these issues in these "globalist", "postcolonial" times, concludes with words that provide a very apt description of the plight of the Iraqi poets discussed in this paper:

Exile is predicated on the existence of, love for, and bond with, one's native place; what is true of all exile is not that home and love of home are lost, but that loss is inherent in the very existence of both.

Regard experiences as if they were about to disappear. What is it that anchors them in reality? What would you save of them? What would you give up? Only someone who has achieved independence and detachment, someone whose homeland is "sweet" but whose circumstances make it impossible to recapture that sweetness, can answer those questions. (Such a person would also find it impossible to derive satisfaction from substitutes furnished by illusion or dogma.)

This may seem like a prescription for an unrelieved grimness of outlook and, with it, a permanently sullen disapproval of all enthusiasm or buoyancy of spirit. Not necessarily. While it perhaps seems peculiar to speak of the pleasures of exile, there are some positive things to be said for a few of its conditions. Seeing "the entire world as a foreign land" makes possible originality of vision. Most people are principally aware of one culture, one setting, one home; exiles are aware of at least two, and this plurality of vision gives rise to an awareness of simultaneous dimensions, an awareness that—to borrow a phrase from music—is *contrapuntal*.[1]

NOTES

CHAPTER ONE—THREE FIGURES: T.S. ELIOT, F.R. LEAVIS, GEORGE ORWELL

1. Eliot's remarks on this subject are categorical. Thus for him education must "develop a wise and large capacity for orthodoxy, to preserve the individual from the solely centrifugal impulse of heresy." *The Criterion*, X, (July 1932), p. 771. Even the administration of education should be in strictly religious hands, "I mean that the hierarchy of education should be a religious hierarchy. The universities are far gone in secularization." "Modern Education and the Classics" in *Essays Ancient and Modern*, p. 161.
2. *Notes towards the Definition of Culture*, p. 104.
3. P. 105.
4. "It is an essential condition of the preservation of the quality of the culture of the minority," he declared, "that it should continue to be a minority culture." P. 110. For this reason, too, Eliot was an advocate of the racist quota system in education whereby, he declared, "there will be room for a proportion of other persons professing other faiths than Christianity." *The Idea of a Christian Society*, (London 1939), p. 62. In fact, Eliot's attitude towards Black, Jewish and other, i.e. non-Anglo-Saxon, cultures, can be described as cultural racism. His vision of the ideal native culture, the re-erection of the organic community, is a "pure" Anglo-Saxon, agrarian society not "invaded," as he termed it, "by foreign races." (See *After Strange Gods*, p. 16).
5. "The device Liberté, Egalité, Fraternité is only the memorial of the time of revolution: Famille, Travail, Patrie has more permanent value", *Christian News Letter*, No 97 (September 3, 1941).

6. "The Civil War was certainly the greatest disaster in the whole of America history: it is just as certainly a disaster from which the country has never recovered, and perhaps never will." *After Strange Gods*, (London 1934), p. 16.

7. "Most of the concepts which might have attracted me in fascism I seem already to have found, in a more digestible form, in the work of Charles Mauras [the leader of the *Action Française*]. I say a more digestible because I think they have a closer applicability to England than those of [Italian] fascism" *The Criterion*, VIII (December 1928), p. 288. Yet Eliot clearly ranked fascism, even in its Italian variety, above any liberal or socialist doctrine. "I end up by reflecting," he stated, "that the development of fascism in Italy may produce very interesting results in ten or twenty years. And that it is a matter of regret that England has no contemporary and indigenous school of political thought since Fabianism, and as an alternative to it." *The Criterion*, VIII, (December 1928), p. 290.

8. "It would perhaps be more natural, as well as in better conformity with the Will of God," he pontificated, "if there were more celibates, and if those who were married had larger families." *The Idea of a Christian Society*, (London 1939), p. 62.

9. *Notes towards the Definition of Culture*, p. 48.

10. "To aim to make everyone share in the appreciation of the more conscious part of culture is to adulterate and cheapen what you give." P. 107.

11. P. 16.

12. PP. 84–85.

13. Take, for example, these typical Eliotic attitudes: "It is a common place that the increase of the electorate, in Britain, is the destruction of Democracy; that with every vote added, the value of every vote diminishes." *The Criterion*, VIII, (October 1928), p. 281. "A real democracy is always a restricted democracy, and can only flourish with some limitation by hereditary rights and responsibilities." *The Criterion*, VIII (October 1928), p. 287. "The governing elite, of the nation, as a whole, would consist of those whose responsibility was inherited with their affluence and position, and whose forces were constantly increased, and often led, by rising individuals of exceptional talent." *Notes towards the Definition of Culture*, p. 17.

14. *Notes towards the Definition of Culture*, pp. 35–36.

15. P. 120.

16. "I have raised this question, however, solely in support of my contention that culture is not merely the sum of several activities, but a *way of life*." P. 14.

17. P. 15.

18. P. 31.

19. P. 18.

20. P. 16

21. P. 36.

22. P. 48.

23. P. 63.

24. P. 91.

25. P. 100.

26. P. 100.

27. P. 108.

28. Francis Mulhern *The Moment of Scrutiny* (New Left Books—London, 1979).
29. "The Rediscovery of Europe" (1942) in *The Collected Essays*, Vol 2, "My Country Right or Left", p. 203.
30. PP. 206–7. In fact, Orwell's strong antipathy to left-wing writers, like his hatred for the left generally, goes back several years to his notoriously anti-socialist and racist book, *The Road to Wigan Pier*, where it appears in clear-cut remarks like:
    > If one faces facts one must admit that nearly everything describable as Socialist litera-ture is dull, tactless, and bad . . . Every writer of consequence and every book worth reading is on the other side . . . The real Socialist writers, the propagandist writers, have always been dull, empty windbags—Shaw, Barbusse, Upton Sinclair, Williams Morris, Waldo Frank, etc." *The Road to Wigan Pier*, (Gollancz, 1937), pp. 215–6.
31. *Inside the Whale and Other Essays*, (Gollancz, 1940), p. 172.
32. PP. 185–6.
33. Moreover, like many of Orwell's other positions, it was contradicted elsewhere by himself. Only the year before he had declared that "no book is genuinely free from political bias. The opinion that art should have nothing to do with politics is itself a political attitude." ("Why I Write" (1947) in *Such, such were the joys*, p. 7) and "that looking back through my work, I see that it is invariably where I lacked a *political* purpose that I wrote lifeless books." P. 11.
34. "Writers and Leviathan" in *Such, such were the joys*, (Harcourt, Brace and Company, 1953), p. 70.
35. P. 71.
36. *Scrutiny*, September 1940, pp. 173–6.
37. *The Collected Essays*, Vol 2, pp. 56–109.

CHAPTER TWO—RAYMOND WILLIAMS: THE END OF THE LINE

1. *Reading and Criticism* (Frederick Muller, 1950), p. ix.
2. P. 30.
3. "Our Debt to Dr. Leavis" in *Critical Quarterly*, No 3, Autumn 1959, pp. 245–7.
4. "Origins of the Present Crisis" in *Toward Socialism* (Collins, 1965), edited by Perry Anderson and Robin Blackburn, p. 11.
5. *Politics and Letters* (NLB—London, 1979), p. 106.
6. P. 107.
7. P. 44.
8. P. 45
9. PP. 51–2
10. P. 52.
11. P. 61.
12. P. 65.
13. F.R. Leavis, "Literary Criticism and Politics" in *Politics and Letters* No's 2 and 3, 1947, p. 59.

14. George Orwell, "Writers and Leviathan" in *Politics and Letters*, No 4, 1948, pp. 37–8.
15. *Politics and Letters*, p. 69.
16. P. 76.
17. *Drama from Ibsen to Eliot*, (Chatto and Windus, 1961), p. 12.
18. P. 12.
19. P. 26.
20. PP. 27–8.
21. *The English Novel from Dickens to Lawrence*, (Chatto and Windus, 1971), p. 28.
22. P. 95.
23. *New Left Review*, No, 67, 1971.
24. *Orwell* (Fontana—London, 1971)
25. P. 22.
26. P. 22.
27. P. 12.
28. For example, Harold Laski's review in *Left News*, March 1937, reprinted in Jeffrey Meyers *George Orwell: The Critical Heritage*, (Routledge and Kegan Paul, 1975), pp. 104–7.
29. Reprinted in J.Meyers, pp. 91–9.
30. "These direct anticipations of *Nineteen Eight-Four* are primarily responses to fascism, and the 're-institution of slavery', which he also sees happening, is based on the Nazi labour-camps. Nothing could be more false than the quite general idea that Orwell returned from Spain a disillusioned socialist, who then gave his energy to warnings against a totalitarian socialist future."
31. P. 70.
32. P. 71.
33. See, for example, the 1946 reviews of the book by Edmund Wilson and Northrop Frye reprinted in J. Meyers, pp. 204–206 and 206–209.
34. P. 74.
35. P. 76.
36. P. 84.
37. PP. 84–5.
38. P. 90.
39. P. 94.
40. *The Country and the City*, (Chatto and Windus, 1973), p. 302.
41. P. 305.

CHAPTER THREE—E.P. THOMPSON AND PERRY ANDERSON: A DEBATE

1. *New Left Review*, No 9, 1961, pp. 24–5
2. "Origins of the Present Crisis" in *Toward Socialism*, edited for the New Left Review by Perry Anderson and Robin Blackburn (Collins—1965), p. 11.
3. *The Poverty of Theory* (Merlin Press, 1978), p. 35.

4. P. 64.

5. "Our best idiom has been protestant, individualist, empirical, disintegrative of universals; our best moralism has been contextual. Our poets have, on occasion, advanced philosophy further than our philosophers. If I who have been formed in this idiom think about problems of determinism and free will, of social process and individual agency, I move not from Spinoza through Marx to Heidegger and Sartre, but I fall into a different kind of medication, conditioned by a literary culture . . ." in "An Open Letter to Leszek Kolakowski" in *The Poverty of Theory*, p. 106.

6. P. 79.

7. PP. 101–2.

8. P. 102.

9. P. 103.

10. P. iii.

11. P. iii.

12. Here are Thompson's own words:

    "I belong to an emancipated political tradition, encapsulated within a hostile national culture which is itself both smug and resistant to intellectuality and failing in self-confidence; and yet I share the same idiom as that of the culture which is my reluctant host; and I share it not only through the habits of a writer but out of preference. This, if I am honest, is myself, my sensibility. Take Marx and Vico and a few European novelists away, and my most intimate pantheon would be a provincial tea-party: a gathering of the English and the Anglo-Irish. Talk of free-will and determinism, and I think first of Milton. Talk of man's inhumanity, I think of Swift. Talk of morality and revolution, and my mind is off with Wordsworth's Solitary. Talk of the problems of self-activity and creative labour in socialist society, and I am in an instant back with William Morris. "An Open Letter to Leszek Kolakowski", p. 109.

    It is no surprise then that, in 1981, when it seemed that he was achieving BBC respectability, and bourgeois press coverage, Thompson hastened to proclaim himself a 'Morrisist and not a Marxist' on the pages of *The Guardian*, although only two years before he had called himself in *The Observer* 'a Marxist (or a Marxist-fragment) in the Labour Party'. But it seems perhaps that the two are, or should be, the same for Thompson.

13. See, for example, the Introduction to the latest collection of Thompson's essays, *Writing by Candlelight* (Merlin, 1980), where he calls upon the feminist, the anti-racist and all other "alternative" movements to "reconnect with an active national political culture"—which, in plain English, means to join the Labour Party. Thompson's degeneration into an apologist for British imperialism comes out very clearly in that collection, particularly in the essay titled, "A Secret State," first published in 1978, where he openly ascribes the cause of the oppression of the Irish people not to the British imperialist occupation, but, incredibly enough, to the Irish working class:

    "Whatever aggravations have been afforded by British politics and by British military presence, the source of the malaise is not to be found in contemporary 'British imperialism' ('British's backyard Vietnam') but in a historic conflict within Ireland itself, and *within the Irish working class.* In such circumstances, the duties of internationalism should be met, not by giving equivocal rhetorical support, from positions of English safety, to the provisionals, but by throwing our arguments, and if need be our bodies, in between." PP. 171–2.

14. "Socialism and pseudo-Empiricism" in *New Left Review*, No 35, 1966, p. 31.
15. P. 32.
16. "Components of the National Culture," *New Left Review*, No. 50, 1968, p. 3.
17. P. 5.
18. P. 6.
19. P. 8.
20. P. 50.
21. P. 51.
22. P. 56.
23. Tom Nairn, *The Left against Europe?* (Penguin, 1973), p. xix.
24. P. 69.
25. PP. 105–6.
26. "The most influential of modern left-wing cultural essays, Raymond Williams' *Culture and Society,* (1958) is in certain respects very simply a socialist revision and representation of Tonnies' thesis. Its very title is almost a translation of *Gemeinschaft and Geselleschaft* (in some ways a better one than Loomis's 'Community and Association'). It surveys the 'scattered seeds' of English *Gemeinschaft* culture and seeks to show how a 'new culture' *has* in fact been both secretly and openly fostered against the tide of *Geselleschaft* . . . Thus, nearly three quarters of a century after Tonnies, in another part of Europe, national left-wing romantics like Williams and Edward Thompson still struggle to escape from their own version of this conservative 'folklore of self-consciousness.'" P. 111.

    In his second book, *The Break-Up of Britain* (New Left Books, 1977), Nairn puts this neo-romantic "left" nationalist movement in a historical perspective. He says:
    "From the late 1950's onwards there has emerged—at the same time as racism, Powellism, and the chain of government debacles—a gathering of historical revision of socialist culture . . . It was originally associated with the early phases of *New Left Review*, and the Campaign for Nuclear Disarmament, and its major intellectual inspiration has arisen from the work of Edward Thompson (above all *The Making of the English Working Class*) and Raymond Williams (above all *Culture and Society*) . . . As a broad intellectual and ideological trend, this has gone under the banner of populist socialism. Yet it is not difficult to perceive it in another perspective, deriving from the comparative history of national movements . . . Odd as it may seem, the deformation of Englishness by her state—history has generated a late but unmistakable variety of left-nationalist popular culture."
27. Raymond Williams, "The British Left" In *New Left Review*, No 30, 1965, p. 26.
28. Perry Anderson, "The Left in the Fifties" in *New Left Review*, No 29, 1965, p. 15.
29. PP. 16–17.
30. P. 17.
31. *New Left Review*, No 1, 1960, p. 26.
32. *New Left Review*, No 6, 1960, p. 21.

CHAPTER FOUR—A NOTE ON CHRISTOPHER CAUDWELL

1. "The increasing division of labour, which includes also its increasing organisation, seems to produce a movement of poetry away from concrete living, so that art appears to be in opposition to work, a creation of leisure. The poet is typically now the solitary individual: his expression, the lyric. The division of labour has led to a class society, in which consciousness has gathered at the pole of the ruling class, whose rule eventually produces the conditions of idleness. Hence, art ultimately is completely separated from work, with disastrous results to both, which can only be healed by the ending of classes. But meanwhile the movement has given rise to a rich development of technique." *Illusion and Reality* (Lawrence and Wishart—London, 1937), p. 28.
2. P. 7.
3. P. 288.
4. PP. 288–9.
5. *Studies in a Dying Culture*, (Bodley Head—London, 1938), p. 15.
6. P. 18.
7. P. 181.
8. Raymond Williams, *Culture and Society 1780–1950*, (Penguin—London, 1976), p. 277.
9. Francis Mulhern, "The Marxist Aesthetics of Christopher Caudwell" *New Left Review*, No 85, 1974, pp. 37–58.
10. P. 58.
11. In "Caudwell", *The Socialist Register*, 1977, pp. 228–276.
12. P. 234.
13. PP. 270–1.

CHAPTER FIVE—JOHN McGRATH AND THE ALTERNATIVE THEATRE MOVEMENT

1. Published by Methuen, London, 1981.
2. P. 2.
3. P. 11.
4. P. 19.
5. P. 31.
6. P. 56.
7. P. 55.
8. P. 59.
9. P. 61.
10. P. 86.
11. "Although man's social life is the only source of literature and art and is incomparably livelier and richer in content, the people are not satisfied with life and demand literature and art as well. Why? Because while both are beautiful, life as reflected in works of

literature and art can and ought to be on a higher plane, more intense, more concentrated, more typical, nearer the ideal, and therefore more universal than actual everyday life." Mao Tse-tung, *Talks at the Yenan Forum on Literature and Art*, (Foreign Languages Press—Peking, 1967), p. 19.

12. In an article which seems to be a condensed version of these talks, McGrath, in fact, categorically states that "bourgeois theatre has created great, valuable works which should be performed and treasured . . . [and that] No doubt good bourgeois plays will continue to be written and performed." ("Theory and Practice of political Theatre" in *Theatre Quarterly*, No 35, Autumn 1979, p. 51). Revealingly, all this gratuitous praise for the bourgeoisie is followed immediately by vulgar anti-communist remarks about the People's Police and the Gang of Four.

13. Nor can McGrath's nebulous concluding remarks about "becoming a part of the complex movement towards a developed, sophisticated but liberating form of socialism (can there be a non-liberating form?) which is happening all over Europe, East and West, and in many other parts of the World" be a substitute for such an analysis, marred as it is initially by the chauvinistic assumption that Europe is the only centre of civilization from which any "sophisticated" socialism can possibly arise and, more importantly, by its incomprehension of the basic fact that this "superior position" of Europe, as part of the imperialist camp, is built upon the exploitation and the oppression of the rest of the world so contemptuously dismissed by the likes of McGrath, and that the revolution which they never fail to pay lip-service to can only take place through the overthrow by the exploited "rest of the world" of the imperialist oppression and slavery of which "Europe, East and West" is an important part.

14. "Better a Bad night in Bootle . . ." an interview with John McGrath in *Theatre Quarterly*, No 19, 1975, p. 40.

15. P. 40

16. *To Present the Pretence* (Methuen—London, 1977) which contains such gems as "Brecht's essays are written in the peculiar and untranslatable style of German philosophy, full of *perilous* (my italics) abstraction, etc.," p. 36 and "there are many excellent people, by no means McCarthyites, who cannot bring themselves to accept that man can be a Communist" etc., p. 38.

17. "The Activist Papers" in *The Worlds*, (Methuen—London, 1980).

18. Itzin, Catherine *Stages in the Revolution* (Methuen—London, 1980), p. 109.

19. P. 172.

20. P. 81.

21. P. 82.

22. P. 87.

23. P. 152.

24. P. 339.

25. P. 337.

26. P. 96.

27. P. 196.

28 "Ambushes for the Audience: Towards a High Comedy of Ideas" interview with Tom Stoppard, *Theatre Quarterly*, No 14, 1974, p. 12.

29. PP. 12–13.

30. "Drama and the Dialectics of Violence" also titled "Edward Bond: The long Road to Lear" interview with Edward Bond in *Theatre Quarterly*, No 5, 1972, p. 9.
31. "Ten Years of Political Theatre, 1968–78", in *Theatre Quarterly*, No 32, 1979, p. 31.

CHAPTER SIX—ISLAMOPHOBIA AND THE INTELLECTUALS

1. Fredrickson, George M. *Racism: A Short History*, (Princeton University Press, 2007), p. 145.

CHAPTER SEVEN—RADICALS, RENEGADES, PUNDITS AND IMPOSTERS: REFLECTIONS ON THE INTERNATIONAL INTELLIGENTSIA

1. Besteman, C. and H. Gusterson, eds., *Why America's Top Pundits are Wrong* (University of California Press – Berkeley, 2005), p. 2.
2. P. 4.
3. PP. 22–3.
4. P. 12.
5. Sokal, Alan and Jean Bricmont *Fashionable Nonsense: Postmodern Intellectuals' Abuse of Science* (Picador—New York, 1998), p. IX.
6. P. X.
7. P. 5.
8. P. 2.
9. P. 12.
10. P. 3.
11. P. 269.
12. P. X.
13. P. XI.
14. P. 16.
15. P. 49.
16. P. 206.
17. P. 207.
18. P. 208. Eric Hobsbawn, "The new threat to history", *New York Review of Books* (16 December, 1993): 62–64 (Reprinted in Eric Hobsbawn, *On History*, London; Weidenfeld and Nicholson, 1997, chapter 1).
19. P. 208.
20. P. 209.
21. P. 211.
22. Said, Edward, *Representations of the Intellectual* (Pantheon Books—New York, 1994), p. XIII.
23. P. XVII.
24. PP. XVII–XVIII.

25. P. 25.
26. P. 29.
27. P. 22.
28. P. 32.
29. P. 37.
30. P. 54.
31. P. 55.
32. P. 55.
33. P. 57.
34. P. 59.
35. P. 91.
36. P. 91.
37. P. 92.
38. P. 107.
39. P. 109.
40. P. 111.
41. P. 111.
42. P. 113.
43. Crossman, Richard, ed., *The God that Failed* (London, 1950), p. 3.
44. P. 4.
45. P. 5.
46. P. 8.
47. P. 9.
48. PP. 9–10.
49. Engerman, David C. "Foreword" to Richard Crossman *The God that Failed* 2001 edition, p. XXXI.
50. Saunders, Frances Stonor *The Cultural Cold War: The CIA and the World of Arts and Letters* (New Press—New York, 1999), p. 63.
51. P. 245.
52. P. 247.
53. Lilla, Mark *The Reckless Mind: Intellectuals in Politics* (New York Review Books—New York, 2001), p. 82.
54. P. 59.
55. P. 96.
56. PP. 149–50.
57. PP. 150–1.
58. P. 153.
59. P. 162, and pp. 184–8.
60. Johnson, Paul *Intellectuals* (Weidenfeld and Nicolson – London, 1988), p. IX.
61. P. 1, the first paragraph.
62. "Foreword" to Ayaan Hirsi Ali *Infidel* (Free Press—New York, 2007), p. XVI.
63. Ali, Ayaan Hirsi *Nomad* (Alfred Knopf – Canada, 2010), p. 201.
64. P. 205.
65. PP. 212–3.
66. P. 213.

CHAPTER EIGHT—POWER AND THE RADICAL ARAB INTELLECTUAL: THREE CASE STUDIES

1. See, for example, these two passages from *Beginnings* (Basic Books—New York, 1975):

    (A) "It is significant that the desire to create an alternative world, to modify or augment the real world through the act of writing (which is one motive underlying the novelistic tradition of the West) is inimical to the Islamic world-view. The Prophet is he who has *completed* a world-view; thus the word *heresy* in Arabic is synonymous with the verb "to innovate" or "to begin." Islam views the world as a plenum, capable of neither diminishment not amplification. Consequently, stories like those in *The Arabian Nights* are ornamental, variations on the world, not completion of it; neither are they lessons, structures, extensions, or totalities designed to illustrate either the author's prowess in representation, the education of a character, or ways in which the world can be viewed and changed.

    Thus even autobiography as a genre scarcely exists in Arabic literature. When it is to be found, the result is wholly special," pp. 81–2.

    (B) "Outside the Judeo-Christian textual tradition—in the Arab-Islamic, for instance—rather different conditions prevail. One of them is *'idjaz* (sic), a concept which describes the uniqueness of the Koran as rendering all other texts impotent by comparison. Thus since the central text is in Arabic, and since, unlike the Gospels or even the Torah, it is given as unitary and complete, textual tradition are essentially supportive, not restorative. All texts are secondary to the Koran, which is inimitable," p. 199.

CHAPTER NINE—MEDITERRANEANISM IN MODERN ARAB CULTURAL THOUGHT

1. Taha Hussain, *Mustaqbal Al-Thaqafa fi Misr* (The Future of Culture in Egypt) 2nd edition, Dar Al-Ma'aref, Cairo. n.d.
2. PP. 18–19.
3. P. 20.
4. P. 20.
5. P. 26.
6. P. 28.
7. PP. 43–50.
8. P. 50.
9. P. 83.
10. P. 44.
11. "To which are we closer: the East or the West?" *Al-Hilal*, Vol. 35, No. 9, 9 July 1927. Reprinted in *East and West: Part I, 19870–1932*, Edited by Mohammed Kamil Al-Khateeb, Ministry of Culture Publication, Damascus, 1991, pp. 287–291.

12. P. 290.

13. P. 291.

14. P. 291.

15. "Hesitation between East and West." In *Today and Tomorrow*, 1928, pp. 229–257. Reprinted in *East and West: Part I, 19870–1932, oP. cit.*, pp. 292–316.

16. PP. 306–7.

17. Salama Mousa, "East is East and West is West and ne'er the Twain shall Meet." *Al-Majala Al-Jadeeda*, No. 1, 7 May 1930. Reprinted in *Al-Khateeb, oP. cit.*, pp. 408–417.

18. See Rasheed Al-Enany, "Tawfiq al-Hakim and the West: A New Assessment of the Relationship." *British Journal of Middle Eastern Studies*, (2002), 27(2), 165–175.

19. As, for example, Sate' Al-Husary, *Abhath Muktara fil Qawmiya Al-Arabiya* (Selected Studies in Arab Nationalism), Center for Arab Unity Studies, Beirut, 1985, pp. 145–156, 166–191.

20. See, for example, Anwar Al-Jundy, *Muhakamat Taha Hussain* (The Trial of Taha Hussain), Dar Al-'Itisam, n.p. , n.d.

21. See, Muhsin Jasim Al-Musawi, *Al-Istishraq fil Fikr Al-Araby* (Orientalism in Arab Thought), The Arab Institute for Studies and Publishing, First Edition, Beirut, 1993, pp. 57, 66–67, 89–110, and George Tarabishi, *Min Al-Nahdha ilal Radda: Tamazzuqat Al-Thaqafa al-Arabiya fi 'Asr Al-'Awlama* (From Renaissance to Reaction: The Tearing Apart of Arab Culture in the Age of Globalism), Dar al-Saqi, Beirut, 2000, pp. 39–45.

22. Salama Mousa, "*Hatha Al-Watan Al-Misri*" (This Egyptian Homeland), reprinted in Anwar Al-Jundy, *Al-Ma'arik Al-Adabiya fi Misr munthu 1914/1939* (Literary Conflicts in Egypt, 1914–1939), Anglo-Egyptian Publishers, Cairo, 1977, pp. 43–44.

23. PP. 65–66.

24. P. 104.

25. See, Ahmad Madhy, "*Salama Mousa wal Falsafa*" (Salama Mousa and Philosophy) in *Al-Falsafa Al-Arabiya Al-Mouasira* (Contemporary Arabic Philosophy), papers presented at the Second Arabic Philosophy Conference, organized held at the University of Jordan, Center for Arab Unity Studies, Beirut, 1988, pp. 333–366, and Mohammad Dakroub, *Rua' Mustaqbaliya fi Fikr Al-Nahda wal Taqaddum wal 'Adala Al-Ijtimaiya* (Future Visions in the Thought of the Renaissance, Progress, and Social Justice), Dar Al-Faraby, Beirut, 2002, pp. 71–100.

26. Mohammad Dakroub, p. 8.

27. See, for example, Jabir Asfour, *Hawamish 'ala Daftar Al-Tanweer* (Notes on the Enlightenment Notebook), Arab Cultural Center, Beirut, 1994, on such figures as Taha Hussain (103–4), Lewis Awadh 198, and Abdul-Aziz Maqalih (183–4), among many others.

28. Collected under the title of *Dirasat fil 'Hadhara* (Studies in Civilization), The Arab Future Publishing House, Cairo, 1989.

29. P. 45.

30. P. 48.

CHAPTER TEN—POETICS OF EXILE AND IDENTITY: THE CASE OF MODERN IRAQI POETRY

1. Said, Edward. *Reflections on Exile* (Harvard University Press, 2002), pp. 185–6.

BIBLIOGRAPHY

Abdul-Ghany, Mustafa. *The Transformations of Taha Hussain* (General Egyptian Book Organization—Cairo, 1990) (in Arabic).

Ahmad, Aijaz. *In Theory* (Verso—London, 1990)

Alawy, Hasan. "Al-Jawahiry: Poems Born of the Civilization of Al-Kufa" in Al-Jawahiry, Khayal Muhammad Mahdi *Al-Jawahiry: The Symphony of Departure* (Publications of the Ministry of Culture in the Syrian Arab Republic: Damascus, 1999), 99–116 (in Arabic).

Al-Attiya, Jalel. *Al-Jawahiry: A Poet of the Twentieth Century* (Al-Jamal Publications—Germany, 1998) (in Arabic).

Al-Dabbagh, Abdulla. "Poetics of Exile and Identity: The Case of Modern Iraqi Poetry", *International Journal of Arabic-English Studies*, 2005, 6, 5–14.

———. "Mediterraneanism in Modern Arab Cultural Thought", *Journal of Mediterranean Area Studies*, 2006, 8,1, 349–366.

Al-Jawahiry, Khayal Muhammad Mahdi. *Al-Jawahiry: The Symphony of Departure* (Publications of the Ministry of Culture in the Syrian Arab Republic: Damascus, 1999) (in Arabic).

Al-Jundy, Anwar. *The Trial of Taha Hussain's Thought* (Dar Al-I'tisam: Cairo, 1984) (in Arabic).

Al-Radhy, Majeed. "Al-Jawahiry between Opposition to Tyranny and Exile", in Al-Jawahiry, Khayal, 1999, 128–150 (in Arabic).

Ali, Ayaan Hirsi. *Nomad* (Alfred Knopf—Canada, 2010).

———. *Infidel* (Free Press—New York, 2007).

Anderson, Perry. "Origins of the Present Crisis", *Towards Socialism*, edited by Perry Anderson and Robin Blackburn (Collins—London, 1965).

———. "The Left in the Fifties", *New Left Review*, No 34, 1965.

————. "Socialism and Pseudo-Empiricism", *New Left Review*, No 35, 1966.

Anonymous. "Grant Aid and Political Theatre 1968–1977", *Wedge*, Summer 1977, 4–8.

Ansorge, Peter. *Disrupting the Spectacle—Five Years of Experimental and Fringe Theatre in Britain* (Pitman—London, 1975).

Arden, John. *To Present the Pretence* (Methuen—London, 1977).

Arnold, G.L. "Britain: The New Reasoners," in *Revisionism*, ed. Leopold Labedz (George Allen and Unwin—London, 1962), 299–312.

Baghdadi, Shawqi. "Al-Jawahiry as a Person and as I Knew Him", Al-Jawahiry, in Al-Jawahiry, Khayal, 1999, 157–163 (in Arabic).

Bennet, G. *The Concept of Empire 1774–1947* (A. and C. Black—London, 1962)

Bentley, Eric. *A Century of Hero-Worship* (Beacon Press—Boston, 1957)

————. *The Life of Drama* (Methuen—London, 1965).

Besteman, C. and H. Gusterson, eds., *Why America's Top Pundits are Wrong* (University of Claifornia Press—Berkeley, 2005).

Bond, Edward. *The Worlds* (Methuen—London, 1980).

————. "Drama and the Dialectics of Violence", *Theatre Quarterly*, No 5, 1972.

Bradbury, M. *The Social Context of Modern English Literature* (Basic Blackwell—Oxford, 1971).

Crossman, Richard, ed., *The God that Failed* (London, 1950).

Caudwell, Christopher. *Illusion and Reality* (Lawrence and Wishart—London, 1946).

————. *Studies in a Dying Culture* (Bodley Head—London, 1938).

————. *Further Studies in a Dying Culture* (Bodley Head—London, 1949).

————. *Romance and Realism* (Princeton University Press—Princeton, 1970).

Clark, Jon et al. (eds.). *Culture and Crisis in Britain in the Thirties* (Lawrence and Wishart—London, 1979).

Clarke, S. et al. *One-Dimensional Marxism: Althusser and the Politics of Culture* (Allison and Busby—London, 1980).

Cornforth, Maurice. "Caudwell and Marxism", *Modern Quarterly*, Vol VI, No 1, 1950–51, 16–33.

Craig, Sandy (ed.). *Dreams and Deconstruction: Alternative Theatre in Britain*, (Amber Lane Press—London, 1980).

Curtis, H. *Three Against the Third Republic* (Princeton University Press—Princeton, 1959).

Draper, Michael. "Christopher Caudwell's Illusion" in *1930's: A Challenge to Orthodoxy*, ed. John Lucas (Harvester—Sussex, 1978)

Dummett, Ann. *A Portrait of English Racism* (Penguin—London, 1934).

Edgar, David. *Destiny* (Methuen—London, 1978).

————. "Ten Years of Political Theatre 1968–1978", *Theatre Quarterly*, No 32, 1979.

————. "Toward a Theater of Dynamic Ambiguities", *Theatre Quarterly*, No 33, 1979.

Edward, H.W. *Labour Aristocracy: Mass Basis of Social Democracy* (Aurora Press—Stockholm, 1978).

Eliot, T.S. *After Strange Gods* (Faber and Faber—London, 1934).

————. *The Idea of a Christian Society* (Faber and Faber—London, 1939).

————. *Notes towards the Definition of Culture* (Faber and Faber—London, 1948).

————. "The Literature of Fascism", *The Criterion*, No 31, December 1928.

————. "Mrs Barnes and Mr Rowse", *The Criterion*, No33, July 1929.

Elsom, John. *Post-War British Theatre* (Routledge and Kegan Paul—London, 1976).

Engerman, David C. "Foreword" to Richard Crossman *The God that Failed*, 2001 edition.

Ensor, R. *England 1870–1914* (Clarendon Press—Oxford, 1936).

Fox, Ralph. *The Novel and the People* (Lawrence and Wishart—London, 1937).

Fredrickson, George M. *Racism: A Short History* (Princeton University Press—Princeton, N.J., 2007).

Gardner, Carl (ed.). *Media, Politics and Culture* (Macmillan—London, 1979).

Gottschalk, Peter and Gabriel Greenberg. *Islamophobia: Making Muslims the Enemy*. (Rowman & Littlefield—Lanham. MD, USA, 2008).

Green, M. "Raymond Williams and Cultural Studies", *Working Papers in Cultural Studies*, Autumn 1976.

Greene, F. *The Enemy: Notes on Imperialism and Revolution* (Jonathan Cape—London, 1970).

Gross, Miriam(ed.). *The World of George Orwell* (Weidenfeld and Nicolson—London, 1971).

Halevy, Elie. *A History of the English People, Vol V* (Unwin—London, 1934).

Hall, John. *The Sociology of Literature* (Longman—London, 1976).

Hall S. and Jefferson, R. (ed.). *Resistance through Ritual* (Hutchinson—London, 1976).

Harrison, J. *The Reactionaries* (Gallancz—London, 1966).

Hobson, J.A. *Imperialism: A Study* (Pott and Co—New York, 1902).

Hoggart, R. *The Uses of Literacy* (Chatto and Windus—London, 1957).

Hovsepian, Nubar. "Connections with Palestine", in Michael Sprinker's *Edward Said: A Critical Reader*, 1992, 5–18.

Itzin, Catherine. *Stages in the Revolution—Political Theatre in Britain since 1986* (Methuen—London, 1980).

———— (ed.). *British Alternative Theatre Directory—1979* (Eastbourne—London, 1979).

Jabran, Sulaiman. *The Combination of Opposites: A Study in the Life and Poetry of Al-Jawahiry* (Dar Al-Faris: Jordan, 2003) (in Arabic).

Johnson, Paul. *Intellectuals* (Weidenfeld and Nicolson—London, 1988).

Keresensky, Oleg. *The New British Drama* (Hamish Hamilton—London, 1977).

Kiernan, V.G. "*Culture and Society*" in *New Reasoner*, Summer, 1959.

Kivel, Paul. *Uprooting Racism: How White People can Work for Racial Justice* (New Society Publishers—Toronto, 2002).

Laing, Dave. *The Marxist Theory of Art* (Harvester—London, 1978).

Lawrence, D.H. *Fantasia of the Unconscious* (Heinemann—London, 1961).

————. *Reflections on the Death of a Porcupine* (Martin Secker—London, 1934).

————. *Movement in European History* (Oxford University Press—London, 1971).

Leavis, F.R. *Mass Civilization and Minority Culture* (Minority Press—Cambridge, 1930).

————. *D.H. Lawrence: Novelist* (Chatto and Windus—London, 1955).

————. *Scrutiny: A Retrospect* (Cambridge University Press—Cambridge, 1963).

———— With Denys Thompson. *Culture and Environment* (Chatto and Windus—London, 1933).

————. *D.H. Lawrence* (Minority Press—Cambridge, 1930).

————. *For Continuity* (Minority Press—Cambridge, 1933).

————. *The Great Tradition* (Chatto and Windus—London, 1948).

————. *New Bearings in English Poetry* (Chatto and Windus—London, 1932).

————. *Revaluation* (Chatto and Windus—London, 1936).

Lewis, C.D. *The Mind in Chains* (Frederick Muller—London, 1937).

Lilla, Mark. *The Reckless Mind: Intellectuals in Politics* (New York Review Books—New York, 2001).

Lodge, David (ed.). *Twentieth-Century Literary Criticism—A Reader* (Longman—London, 1972).

Margolies, D.N. *The Function of Literature: A Study of Christopher Caudwell's Aesthetics* (International Publishers—New York, 1969).

Meyers, J. *George Orwell—The Critical Heritage* (Routledge and Kegan Paul—London, 1969).

McGrath, John. *A Good Night out—Popular Theatre, Audience, Class and Form* (Methuen—London, 1981).

————. "The Theory and Practice of Political Theatre", *Theatre Quarterly*, No 35, 979, 43–55.

————. "Better a Bad Night Bootle . . ." *Theatre Quarterly*, No 19, 1975, 39–55.

————. "Boom: An Introduction", *New Edinburgh Review*, No 30, 1975.

Mirsky, D. *The Intelligentsia of Great Britain* (Gollancz—London, 1935).

Mulhern, Francis. *The Moment of 'Scrutiny'* (New Left Books—London, 1979).

————. "The Marxist Aesthetics of Christopher Caudwell" *New Left Review*, No 85, 1974, 37–58.

Munif, Abdul- Rahman. "Al-Jawahiry's Journey and Departure: The Legend of a Century", in *Al-Jawahiry*, Khayal, 1999, 226–232 (in Arabic).

Nabudere, Dan. *The Political Economy of Imperialism* (Zed Press—London, 1977).

Nairn, Tom. *The Left against Europe?* (Penguin—London, 1973).

————. *The Break-up of Britain* (New Left Books—London, 1977).

Nietzsche, F. *Beyond Good and Evil* (Allen and Unwin—London, 1967).

————.*The Will to Power* (Weidenfeld and Nicolson—London, 1968).

Nightingale, Benedict. *An Introduction to 50 Modern British Plays* (Pan Books—London, 1982).

No Author. *Essays on Socialist Realism and The British Cultural Tradition* (Arena—London, n.d.).

Orwell, George. *The Road to Wigan Pier* (Gollancz—London, 1937).

————. *Homage to Catalonia* (Secker and Warburg—London, 1938).

————. *The Lion and the Unicorn* (Secker and Warburg—London, 1941).

————. *Animal Farm* (Secker and Warburg—London, 1945).

————. *Nineteen Eight-Four* (Secker and Warburg—London, 1949).

————. *Such, such were the Joys* (Harcourt, Brace and World—New York, 1953).

————. *The Collected Essays, Journalism and Letters of George Orwell—4 volumes* (Harcourt, Brace and World—New York, 1968).

Rattansi, Ali. *Racism.* (Oxford University Press: Oxford, 2007).

Ray, Paul C. *The Surrealist Movement in Britain* (Cornell University Press—Ithaca, 1971).

Robbins, Russell Hope. *The T.S. Eliot Myth* (Henry Schuman—New York, 1951).

Said, Edward. *Beginnings* (Basic books: New York, 1975).

————. *Representations of the Intellectual* (Pantheon Books—New York, 1994)

————. *Out of Place: A Memoir* (New York, Knopf—New York, 2000).

————. *The Pen and the Sword: Dialogues with David Barsamian*, translated into Arabic by Tawfiq Al-Asadi, (Dar Kana'an—Damascus, 2004).

Sammers, Jeffrey. *Literary Sociology and Practical Criticism* (Indiana University Press—Bloomington, 1977).

Schumpeter, J. *Imperialism and Social Classes* (A.M. Kelly—New York, 1951).

Semmel, B. *Imperialism and Social Reform* (G. Allen and Unwin—London, 1960).

Seyd, R. "The Theatre of Red Ladder", *New Edinburgh Review*, No 30, 1975.

Sokal, Alan and Jean Bricmont. *Fashionable Nonsense: Postmodern Intellectuals' Abuse of Science* (Picador—New York, 1998).

Sprinker, Michael. *Edward Said: A Critical Reader* (Blackwell: Oxford, 1992).

Saunders, Francis Stonor. *The Cultural Cold War: The CIA and the World of Arts and Letters* (New Press—New York, 1999).

Stoppard, Tom. "Ambushes for The Audience: Towards a High Comedy of Ideas", *Theatre Quarterly*, No 14, 1974.

Strachey, J. *The Coming Struggle For Power* (Gollancz—London, 1932).

Styan,J.L. *Modern Drama in Theory and Practice—3volumes* (Cambridge University Press—Cambridge, 1981).

Swingewood, A. *The Myth of Mass Culture* (Macmillan—London, 1977).

Thompson, E.P. "Caudwell", *The Socialist Register*, 1977, 228–276.

———. *The Poverty of Theory* (Merlin Press—London, 1978).

———. *Writing by Candlelight* (Merlin Press—London, 1980).

———. "Socialism and the Intellectuals", *Universities and Left Review*, No 1, Spring, 1957.

———. "Socialism and the Intellectuals", *Universities and Left Review*, No 2, Summer, 1957.

———. "Socialist Humanism", *The New Reasoner*, No 1, Summer, 1957.

———. "The Long Revolution", *New Left Review*, No's 9, 10, 11, 1961.

Thomson, George. "İn Defence of Poetry", *Modern Quarterly*, Vol VI, No 2, Spring 1951, 107–134.

Trussler, Simon. *New Theatre Voices of the Seventies* (Methuen—London, 1981).

Watson, Garry. *The Leavises, The "Social" and the Left* (Brynmill—London, 1977).

West, Alick. *Crisis and Criticism* (Lawrence and Wishart—London, 1975).

———. "On 'Illusion and Reality'", *Communist Review*, January 1948, 7–13.

Widgery, David. *The Left in Britain, 1956–1968* (Penguin—London, 1976).

Williams, Raymond. "Our Debt to Dr Leavis", *Critical Quarterly*, No 3, Autumn, 1959.

———. "Literature and Sociology—In Memory of Lucien Goldmann", *New Left Review*, No 67, 1971.

———. "The British Left", *New Left Review*, No 30, 1965.

———. *Reading and Criticism* (Frederick Muller—London, 1966).

———. *Drama from Ibsen to Eliot* (Penguin—London, 1964).

———.*Culture and Society 1780–1950* (Pelican—London, 1976).

———. *The Long Revolution* (Pelican—London, 1975).

———.*Modern Tragedy* (Chattoand Windus—London, 1966).

———. *Drama from Ibsen to Brecht* (Chatto and Windus—London, 1971).

———. *Orwell* (Fontana—London, 1975).

———. *The English Novel from Dickens to Lawrence* (Chatto and Windus—London, 1971).

———. *The Country and the City* (Chatto and Windus—London, 1973).

———. *Marxism and Literature* (Oxford University Press—London, 1977).

———. *Politics and Letters.* (New Left Books—London, 1979).

———. *Problems in Materialism and Culture* (New Left Books—London, 1980).

Studies on Themes and Motifs in Literature

The series is designed to advance the publication of research pertaining to themes and motifs in literature. The studies cover cross-cultural patterns as well as the entire range of national literatures. They trace the development and use of themes and motifs over extended periods, elucidate the significance of specific themes or motifs for the formation of period styles, and analyze the unique structural function of themes and motifs. By examining themes or motifs in the work of an author or period, the studies point to the impulses authors received from literary tradition, the choices made, and the creative transformation of the cultural heritage. The series will include publications of colloquia and theoretical studies that contribute to a greater understanding of literature.

For additional information about this series or for the submission of manuscripts, please contact:

Dr. Heidi Burns
Peter Lang Publishing
P.O. Box 1246
Bel Air, MD 21014-1246

To order other books in this series, please contact our Customer Service Department:

800-770-LANG (within the U.S.)
212-647-7706 (outside the U.S.)
212-647-7707 FAX

Or browse online by series at:

www.peterlang.com